Illustrated Biography of

WILLIAM
SHAKESPEARE

Illustrated Biography of

WILLIAM
SHAKESPEARE

Manju Gupta
Azeem Ahmad Khan

GENERAL PRESS
New Delhi

Published by
GENERAL PRESS
4228/1, Second Floor
Ansari Road, Daryaganj
New Delhi – 110002
Ph.: 23282971, 45795759
e-mail: generalpressindia@gmail.com

First Edition: 2018

ISBN : 9789387669246

Purchase our books online from:
www.amazon.in
www.flipkart.com

Published by Azeem Ahmad Khan for General Press
Printed at Repro Knowledgecast Limited, Thane

CONTENTS

PART II

INTRODUCTION

William Shakespeare (1564-1616), recognised as one of English literature's greatest influences known, has left behind more than a million words of text. He was a respected poet and playwright though his reputation did not rise to its present heights until the 19th century. Yet, very little is known about him and his personal life. After 400 years of dedicated searching and hunting, researchers have found about 100 documents relating to his personal life and these include his baptismal records, title deeds, tax certificates, marriage bonds, writs of attachment, court records and his tombstone. However, "they tell us a great deal about the business of a person's life, but almost nothing about the emotions of it," says Bill Bryson, who is the international best-selling author of *The Lost Continent.*

During his lifetime no biography was ever written of William Shakespeare. Thus too little can be factually supported of what we believe to be the events of his life. Considered the greatest playwright that the world has ever known, William Shakespeare was no less a poet to write in English language and for which he is often known as "The Bard" or the "Bard of Avon". He is also the most popular playwright as no one else's plays have been produced so many times or read so widely in so many countries. The Romantics, in particular, acclaimed Shakespeare's genius and the Victorians hero-worshipped him with a reverence that George Bernard Shaw called "bardolatry". In the 20th century, his works were repeatedly adopted and rediscovered by new movements in scholarship and performance. His plays remain highly popular today and are consistently performed and reinterpreted in diverse cultural and political contexts throughout the world. Anecdotes and criticisms written by his rivals pay him tributes as the greatest playwright, poet and actor.

Many reasons can be given for Shakespeare's broad appeal but the main one is essentially his understanding of human nature. He could see in a specific dramatic situation the qualities that relate to all human beings. Also he could see the human aspect of any dramatic situation as he created characters which were so real and familiar. Not being symbolic figures, the characters were highly individualistic who were struggling in life, at times successfully and at others, painfully as tragic failures.

Apart from his understanding of human nature, he had knowledge of a wide variety of subjects like music, art, politics, stage, military science, the Bible, law, history, hunting and sports. Yet, he is supposed to possess no professional experience in any field except the theatre. His surviving works comprise thirty-eight plays, which are divided into comedies, histories and tragedies, 154 sonnets, two long narrative poems and several other poems. His plays have been translated into most of the major languages of the world and performed more often than the plays of any other playwright. The characters in his plays are drawn from all walks of life—from kings to misers, from generals to drunkards, from philosophers to shepherds, from jesters to hired killers.

He took birth in a middle-class family in the small market town of Stratford-upon-Avon, married at eighteen and went to participate in the theatrical world of London. It took no time for him to become the city's leading actor and playwright. He wrote essentially comedies and historical plays during the initial years of his life in London. These were the two genres which he raised to the peak of sophistication and artistry with a deft handling of his pen and imagination. His exceptional portrayal of historical figures, like Julius Caesar and Mark Antony is quite different and enlightening in comparison to what history tells us.

His style of writing and ability to coin words helped to shape the literature of many European countries, not to mention his homeland. His ability to innovate and mould the words into a live language prevented English language from becoming stilted or stagnant. Some of the phrases used by Shakespeare have come into such common use that one can hear even today someone saying, "If music be the food of love, play on…" or "Friends, Romans, countrymen, lend me your ears…" He could express the most simplest of ideas and incidents in the most colourful language, making drab ordinary events appear like great happenings. As an example, when talking of jealousy, Shakespeare described it as a "green-eyed monster which does mock the meat it feeds on", in his tragedy entitled *Othello*.

Writers, poets and dramatists have earned worldwide fame and glory but Shakespeare's works have generated a never-ending curiosity and interest, leaving an indelible impact on the literary world of today. Few records of Shakespeare's private life survive and speculation continues about such matters as his sexuality, religious beliefs and whether the works attributed to him were written by him or others.

Shakespeare's popularity can be attributed to his creative genius in writing plays that to this day appeal to readers as well as theatre-goers. His work has been translated and reprinted innumerable number of times; his plays have not only been performed repeatedly on stage, but consistently adapted and rediscovered by new movements in scholarly performance. Movies like *Hamlet* and *Macbeth* have been made on the basis of his plays and composers have written operas and musical comedies using his stories and characters as the foundation. Later he switched over to writing tragicomedies or romances for which he collaborated with fellow playwrights.

Some of the words which are read by millions of people without realising that it was Shakespeare who had created them are as follows: amazement, birthplace, cold-blooded, dawn, eyeball, fashion-able, generous, ill tempered, jaded, love letter, majestic, outgrow, puppy dog, quarrelsome, rascally, schoolboy, tranquil, useful, vulnerable, well-behaved, yelping, zany, etc. His phrases often heard being used by us all are: "All the world's a stage, and all the men and women merely players…" from *As You Like It*; "Knock, knock, knock! Who's there?" from *Macbeth*; "Neither a borrower, nor a lender be…" from *Hamlet*; "Parting is such sweet sorrow…" from *Romeo and Juliet*; "Neither rhyme nor reason…" from *The Comedy of Errors*; "To thine own self be true…" from *Hamlet*; "Too much of a good thing…" from *As You Like It*; "Wild goose chase…" from *Romeo and Juliet*, etc.

PART I

SHAKESPEARE'S FAMILY TREE

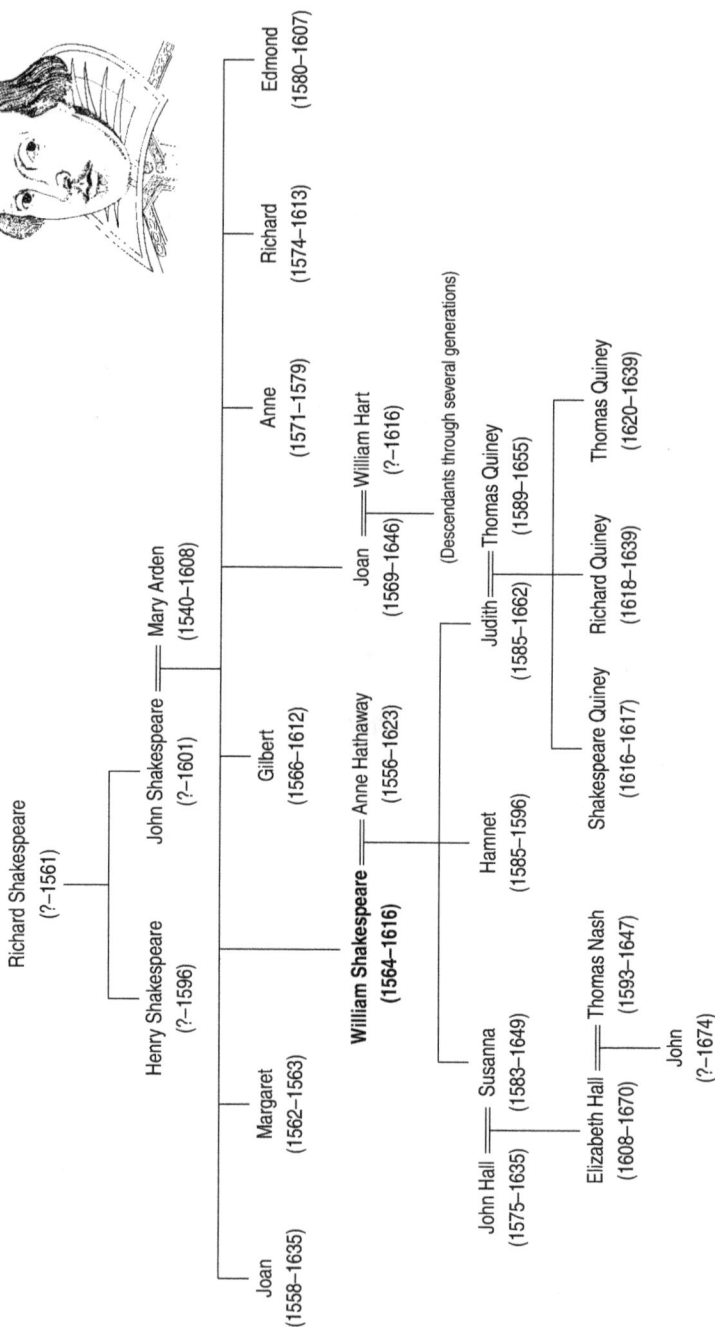

Richard Shakespeare
(?–1561)

Henry Shakespeare
(?–1596)

John Shakespeare — Mary Arden
(?–1601)   (1540–1608)

Joan
(1558–1635)

Margaret
(1562–1563)

Gilbert
(1566–1612)

Anne
(1571–1579)

Richard
(1574–1613)

Edmond
(1580–1607)

William Shakespeare — Anne Hathaway
(1564–1616)   (1556–1623)

Joan = William Hart
(1569–1646)   (?–1616)

(Descendants through several generations)

Susanna — John Hall
(1583–1649) (1575–1635)

Hamnet
(1585–1596)

Judith — Thomas Quiney
(1585–1662)   (1589–1655)

Elizabeth Hall = Thomas Nash
(1608–1670)   (1593–1647)

John
(?–1674)

Shakespeare Quiney
(1616–1617)

Richard Quiney
(1618–1639)

Thomas Quiney
(1620–1639)

Chapter 1

Early Life

Birth

William Shakespeare is also spelled as Shakspere, Shaksper and Shake-spears as spellings in Elizabethan times were liable to change. What is more, the Englishperson of the time bothered little about maintaining biographical information which had nothing to do with either the church or the State. It could also have been possible that his countrymen did not realise his capability and eminence as a leading playwright or maybe they looked down upon mere dramatists.

Though recognised as one of literature's greatest influences, very little is known about William Shakespeare. Whatever is known has been culled from registrar's records, court records, wills, marriage certificate and his tombstone. The register of Holy Trinity, the parish church in Stratford, records that William Shakespeare's baptism was done on Wednesday, April 26th, 1564. Since the infants at that time were baptised three days after their birth, it is generally accepted that Shakespeare was born on April 23rd, which happened to be St. George's Day.

Let us look at the picture of the world into which William was born. Queen Elizabeth I had been queen for six years. She was thirty-one-years old with no interest in war. Under "Good Queen Bess", as Elizabeth was popularly known, England grew more and more prosperous.

Artists in Europe, especially in Italy, were creating some of the most beautiful paintings and sculptures the world had ever seen. The printing press, invented in the 1400s, had made many more books available. Earlier the books had to be copied by hand. More and more people had taken to learning to read and write. In 1514, Nicolaus Copernicus, a Polish astronomer, first wrote that the sun was the centre of the universe. Prior to that people believed that the Earth was the centre around which the sun and other planets circled. It was also the time of discovery of new places and ideas. In 1519, Ferdinand Magellan, a Portuguese explorer, set out to sail all around the world. The trip took him three years.

Parents and Siblings

William Shakespeare was born in Stratford, which had only eight or nine streets and fewer than 1,500 inhabitants. It was a market town, where the local farmers could bring their crops, animals and other goods to sell. William was the third child of John and Mary Shakespeare, who had eight children in all. The first two were daughters, Joan (1558-1635) and Margaret (1562-1563), before William. Joan married a local hatter named Hart and lived to be seventy-seven. Gilbert (1566-1612) was born after William who became a successful haberdasher. Then came another daughter, also named Joan (1569-1646), who was followed by Anne (1571-1579),

Richard (1574-1613) and Edmund (1580-1607). Edmund became an actor in London but how successful he was is not known as he died at the age of twenty-seven. He is buried in Southwark Cathedral, the only one of the eight siblings not to rest at Holy Trinity in Stratford.

William's eldest living sister, Joan, outlived her famous playwright brother. Thus out of his seven siblings, only one sister and four of his brothers survived to reach adulthood.

The Shakespeare family enjoyed considerable local prominence. William's father, John, is often said to have been illiterate. Illiteracy was the usual condition in the 16th-century England, because according to one estimate, at least 70 per cent of men and 90 per cent of women of the period couldn't even pronounce their names. Literary or not, John was a popular and respected fellow. In 1556, he took up the first of the many municipal positions when he was elected borough-ale taster. Two years later he became a constable—a position that, as now, argued for some physical strength and courage. The next year he became an "affeeror", one who assessed fines for matters not handled by existing statutes. By 1560, he was one of the fourteen burgesses which constituted the town council. In 1565, John became an alderman and three years later, he was elected bailiff (mayor), the highest civic honour that a Stratford resident could achieve. His authority was symbolised by an ornamental staff called a mace. This was carried before him in processions by an officer, called a sergeant-at-mace. This was in 1568 by when he had become a local businessman, who dabbled in tanning, leather work and whittawering (a process in which white or soft leather is tanned to make items like purses and gloves). He also dealt in grain and was often described as a glover by trade.

John was eligible for a coat of arms and applied to the College of Heralds for one, but his worsening financial status prevented him from obtaining it. It is said that later he held several other civic posts but in 1576, something severely unpleasant seems to have taken place in his business life, possibly participation in black market of wool. When his son, William, was twelve-years old, he abruptly withdrew from public affairs and stopped attending meetings.

John Shakespeare successfully renewed his application for the coat of arms in 1596, most probably at the instigation of William himself, as he was more prosperous at the time. However, as an actor, William was not eligible and the application still relied on his father's qualification. It wasn't enough to be well-off in Shakespeare's England. To move up in social class and to be thought of as gentlemen, men wanted to acquire a coat of arms. It was a shield-shaped design that bore the Shakespeare family motto that read:

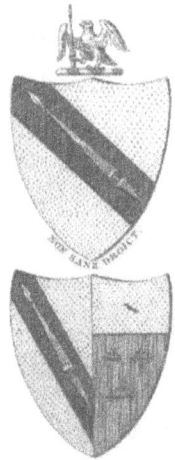

Shakespeare's coat of arms

"*non sanz droit*" in Latin, meaning, "not without right". It showed a certain defensiveness and insecurity on the part of its author, most likely William. It is thus no surprise that the theme of social status and restoration runs deep through the plots of many of Shakespeare's plays and seems to mock his own longing.

A coat of arms was usually granted based on family status and noble deeds but sometimes it was bought at a high price. Once John Shakespeare was granted a coat of arms, he could pass it down to William and future generations of the Shakespeares.

John was listed among the nine Stratford residents who were thought to have missed church services "for fear of processe for debtte". He even lost his position as an alderman. His colleagues repeatedly reduced or excused levies that he owed to them. They also kept his name on the roll for another ten years in the hope that he would make a recovery. He never did. When he died in 1601, he left William only a little real estate.

William's mother was Mary Arden, a daughter of the gentry. She married John Shakespeare in 1557 and set up house at Henley Street, some 100 miles northwest of London. She came from a minor branch of a

William was born in this house

prominent family. Her father farmed and the family was comfortable, but probably no more than that. Apparently she came from a wealthier family than her husband. Being the youngest daughter in her parental family, she inherited much of her father's landowning and farming estate after his death. Some evidence points to possible Roman Catholic sympathies on both sides of the family. It is said that the Ardens were Roman Catholics but Shakespeare publicly belonged to the Church of England, the State church.

Boyhood and Schooling

Stratford-upon-Avon, in Warwickshire, is called the heart of England and was well farmed and heavily wooded. The town itself was not only prosperous and progressive, but proud of its King

Edward's New School, a free grammar school. The king, honoured in the school's name, had nothing to do with the original founding of the school which had Roman Catholic origins.

Some say that at about the age of four, William would have gone to a "petty school" to learn to read. It was a small private school for boys and girls. At six, girls left the petty school to be taught at home by their mothers or, if they were rich, by private tutors. At the same age, if their parents could afford not to send them out to work, sons of middle-class men, like John Shakespeare, were given free education at the local grammar school.

The school was chartered in 1553 and was situated about a quarter mile away from his home. Young William went to it with other boys of his social class, though when or for how long is not known. He may have been a pupil of the school from his seventh to thirteenth years.

Grammar schools varied in quality during the Elizabethan era, but the curriculum was dictated by law throughout England. It is quite possible the school provided intensive education in Latin grammar and the classics. Knowledge of Latin was necessary for a career in medicine, law or the church. Besides, Latin was considered a sign of education. William probably began learning it when he was seven. Church services were held in Latin; laws were written in Latin. As William grew older, he and the other boys were not allowed to speak in English at school and if they did, they were spanked. William learned not only Latin grammar, he knew famous speeches in Latin by heart and he could write in Latin. Students spent about nine hours daily at school, attending classes the year round except for their brief holiday period.

It is assumed that young William learned to read from a hornbook—a board with the letters of the alphabet and the Lord's Prayer printed on it. He also learned many other prayers. He may have read outstanding ancient Roman authors as Cicero, Ovid, Plautus, Seneca, Terence and Virgil. One of William Shakespeare's earliest plays, *The Comedy of Errors*, bears similarity to Plautus's *The Two Menaechmuses* which could well have been staged at school.

Hornbook

Four of the six schoolmasters at the school during William's boyhood were graduates of Oxford University and were Catholic sympathisers. Simon Hunt, who was likely to have been one of William's teachers, later became a Jesuit.

By modern standards, the Stratford grammar school must have been demanding, dull and strict. There is no evidence available to show that there could have been a teacher who could have stirred his imagination and made routine studies interesting.

On the basis of the plays Shakespeare has written, it has been assumed that he must have learned early about the woods and fields, about birds, insects and small animals. The fields and woods around Stratford provided opportunities to hunt and trap small game. River Avon running through the town had enough fish to catch. William's writings reveal accurate descriptions of flowers, trees, wild birds and animals, clouds and the changing seasons,

The 16th century was a time of bitter religious divisions. All English people were Christian, but there were two rival versions of the faith—Catholicism and Protestantism. In 1534, King Henry VIII broke with the Catholic Church and declared himself head of the Anglican or English Church. Under his son Edward VI (1547-53), the Anglican Church became Protestant. There was a swing back to Catholicism under Queen Mary (1553-58) but Queen Elizabeth restored Protestantism (1588-1603), fining anyone who refused to worship in an Anglican Church. The Protestants were split into Anglicans and Puritans. The latter wanted to strip away all features of Christian worship that did not appear in the Bible. They thought that the Anglican Church should get rid of bishops, vestments, or church clothes and all elaborate ceremonies, which they called "Popish practices". Many Puritans rejected the use of the crucifix, a cross depicting the crucifixion of Christ, as a Christian symbol. They disapproved of jewelled crosses.

In 1587, Queen Elizabeth had her cousin, Mary Stuart, Queen of Scots, executed. Mary, a Catholic, was kept a prisoner in England since 1568, when she fled from Scotland after being defeated in battle by the Scottish Protestants. She was beheaded after becoming the focus of a series of plots by

Plots against the queen

English Catholics. They had planned to murder Elizabeth and replace her with Mary. Such plots were encouraged by the Pope, the head of the Catholic Church, who had declared in 1570 that Elizabeth was no longer the rightful queen.

which undoubtedly are based upon his childhood experiences and love of the countryside. In *Macbeth*, William Shakespeare describes night falling with the words: "Light thickens, and the crow makes wing to the rooky wood." In *Romeo and Juliet*, Capulet, hearing of his daughter's death, says, "Death lies on her like an untimely frost upon the sweetest flower in all the fields." He uses images of crops, plants and wild flowers to bring his writing to life. In *Hamlet*, the mad Ophelia makes "fantastic garlands" of "crow flowers, nettles, daisies and long purples". The wicked queen in *Cymbeline* sends her ladies to gather violets, cowslips and primroses, in order to make poison.

William knew something about trade and outdoor sports too. He must have gathered enough about hunting, hawking, fishing, dance, music and other arts and sports. In *Henry VI*, Part Three, Queen Margaret compares the enemies pursuing her to two greyhounds: "Edward and Richard, like a brace of greyhounds having the fearful fleeing hare in sight… are at our back." A Lord in *The Taming of the Shrew* asks the question, "Dost thou love hawking?" William Shakespeare certainly did as he mentions it more often in his plays than he did any other sport. When the heroine of *Romeo and Juliet* wants to call back her departing lover, she cries, "O! For a falconer's voice, to lure this tassel-gentle back again." A "tassel-gentle" was a name for a male peregrine falcon. William Shakespeare's Scottish king, Macbeth, compares himself to a baited bear: "They have tied me to the stake; I cannot fly, but bear-like I must stay and fight the course."

Shakespeare also seemed to know about alchemy, astrology, folklore, medicine and law. This information could have either been collected by reading books or through daily observation of the world around him. There is no evidence that his education extended beyond the grammar school. This lack of evidence makes one presume that William, whose works are today studied usually at universities, never attended one himself.

Despite the long hours spent at school, William's boyhood was probably not confined to studies alone. As a market centre, Stratford was a lively town. In addition, holidays provided pageants and shows, including plays about the legendary outlaw Robin Hood and his merry men. By 1569, travelling companies of professional actors were free going in Stratford, which held two large fairs every year, attracting visitors from other countries too. Moreover, the nearby town of Coventry was famous for staging mystery plays based on stories from the Bible. Stages were set up on wagons. A different scene from the mystery play was performed on each wagon as they rolled through. People came to Coventry from all over to watch. Perhaps, young William travelled there to see them.

William's father John liked actors and as high bailiff, he gave

Players performing in an inn yard

the professional actors permission to perform in town. He paid them 9 shillings from the Stratford treasury to put on a show. That was a lot of money then. The plays were performed in town halls, inns and squares mainly. There were no theatres. William must have watched the actors build stages in the town square and hang thick rolls of fabric for backdrops before pulling out fancy costumes from their trunks for the play to begin. William must have been spellbound at sword fights, battles, love scenes, tears and laughter. It must have been pure magic for a youngster like him!

Moreover, traders came to London from all over the world to buy and sell goods—gold from Africa, silks and spices from Venice, tobacco from America, hand-painted wallpaper from China. Moreover, as William ate supper in crowded inns, he mingled with people from faraway places who had different news to give. Lectures were a popular pastime. William could hear explorers and scientists describe their travels and discoveries. And as he shared glasses of ale with soldiers in noisy taverns, he enjoyed tales of England's recent victory over Spain. However, there are some historians who counter that for young William, Stratford could not have been an exciting place to live in.

Physical Appearance

Although it is difficult to tell from the portraits that survive, William Shakespeare might have been considered quite handsome in his days. His most famous likeness—the one that appears on souvenir bags and on book covers, is known as the "Droeshout engraving". The face seems somehow a little too somber and stiff for a clever man like Shakespeare to be.

We have no written description of William Shakespeare penned in his own lifetime The first textual portrait saying, "He was a handsome, well-shap't man: very good company, and of very readie and pleasant smooth witt" was written sixty-four years after his death by a man, John Aubrey, who was born ten years after Shakespeare's death.

Marriage and Children

At the age of eighteen, he married the twenty-six-year old Anne Hathaway, who bore him three children. William Shakespeare married the pregnant Anne Hathaway on November 28th, 1582. Anne was the daughter of a yeoman farmer, Richard Hathaway, who lived in Shottery, a village about a mile from Stratford. Richard Hathaway died in September 1581, bequeathing Anne a sum of 6 pounds, 13 shillings and 4 pence to be paid "at the day of her marriage". From the difference in their ages, it was rumoured

Hathaway's house

that William and Anne were unhappy together. Some historians say that this was a "shotgun wedding" forced on a reluctant William by the Hathaway family. There is, however, no reliable evidence for this inference.

Here it may be pointed out that the age difference between William and Anne was typical of couples of that time. Women, such as the orphaned Anne, often stayed at home to care for younger siblings and married in the late twenties, often to younger eligible men. Furthermore a "handfast" marriage and pregnancy were frequent precursors to legal marriages at the time. Certainly William was bound to marry her having made her pregnant, but there is no reason to assume that that had not always been his intention. It is likely the bride and groom's families had known one another and forged the alliance.

The marriage is supported by documents from the Episcopal Register at Worcester, which records in Latin the issuing of a wedding licence to "Wm Shaxpere" and one "Anne Whatley" of Temple Grafton. A day afterwards, Fulk Sandells and John Richardson, relatives of Hathaway from Stratford, signed a surety of 40 pounds as a financial guarantee for the wedding of "Willam Shagspere and Anne Hathawey". Frank Harris, in *The Man Shakespeare* (1909), argues that these documents were evidence that Shakespeare was involved with two women. He had chosen to marry Whatley, but when this became known, he was immediately forced by Hathaway's family to marry their pregnant relative. According to the *Oxford Companion to Shakespeare*, most modern scholars take the view that the name Whatley was "almost certainly the result of clerical error."

The playwright's marriage to Anne Hathaway may have been officiated, amongst other candidates, by John Frith in the town of Temple Grafton, a few miles from Stratford. Some surmise that Shakespeare wed in Temple Grafton rather than the Protestant Church in Stratford so that the wedding could be performed as a Catholic sacrament. The couple may have arranged the marriage in haste since the Worcester Chancellor allowed the marriage banns to be read once, instead of the usual three times or probably Anne's pregnancy was the reason for this.

Six months after her marriage, Anne gave birth to a daughter Susanna who was baptised on May 26th, 1583. On February 2nd, 1585, twins, a son Hamnet and daughter Judith, followed and were baptised. But Hamnet died of unknown causes at the age of eleven and was buried on August 11th, 1596. Hamnet and Judith were named after William's close friends, Judith and Hamnet Sadler. William's family was unusually small in an era when many children were given birth to ensure that parents were cared for in later years, what with the high mortality rates of children and the life expectancy in the 1500s.

Following the birth of the twins, there are few historical traces of William. Indeed, the period from 1585 (when his three children were born) to 1592, when due to his twenty years of life apart from Anne and brief mention of her in his will, it is assumed that this was not a happy marriage. Anne never left Stratford, living there her entire life.

Chapter 2

Lost Years

No one really knows when Shakespeare first came to London. Ever a shadow even in his own biography, he disappears, all but utterly, from 1585-1592, the very years when we would like to know where he was and what he was up to, for it was in this period that he left Stratford and established himself as an actor and playwright. Looking for work in London, just four days' ride from Stratford, William is believed to have left his family back home for some twenty years while he pursued his craft.

According to one story, William had to flee from Stratford after being caught poaching deer in Sir Thomas Lucy's deer park. This story comes from William Shakespeare's first biography, written in 1709 by John Rowe. He based his book on tales the Stratford people were telling about the playwright. Some scholars believe that some time during the lost years Shakespeare moved to London and served a period of apprenticeship in the city's busy theatrical life.

William was just one of the thousands of the country people who moved to the great city in the late 16th century. He found himself in a bustling, crowded place with narrow, dark streets littered with all sorts of rubbish. As a newcomer, Shakespeare would have been struck by the noise, the dirt and the smells of the city. Crossing London Bridge, he might have been shocked by the sight of the heads of executed traitors rotting on poles. He could have been impressed by the beauty of the grand churches and the riverside mansions of London's wealthy merchants and nobles.

William only returned back to his family in 1609, having visited only during the effort-day period of Lent when theatres, though open well into the start of Lent, would later close in accordance with the traditional banning of all forms of diversionary entertainment around this important Easter event. Having grown up in sleepy Stratford, William must have found London an exciting place to live in. It was the largest city in northern Europe and ten times the size of any other English town. Even before the

City of London at the time of Shakespeare

playhouses were built, London had many different entertainments to offer its citizens.

Londoners enjoyed watching cruel blood-sports, such as fights between bulls, bears and packs of dogs and they often gathered to watch executions. Many people passed their time by gambling at dice and cards or playing sports, such a bowls. London was full of criminals who made a living by cheating at cards and dice. These cheats were called coneycatchers, who were on the lookout to trap newcomers to town.

For hundreds of years, scholars have hunted for clues that might explain what William Shakespeare was doing during his lost years. His writing shows knowledge of different types of work including medicine (this is somewhat doubtful because, though his work shows knowledge of medicine, his characters are often scornful of physicians or doctors. Macbeth says, "Throw physico to the dogs" and Timon of Athens says, "Trust not the physician", soldiering (in the 1800s, scholar H.J. Thoms argued that Shakespeare's military knowledge meant that he had served as a soldier. Thoms found a document naming a soldier called William Shakespeare, but this man served in 1605, when Shakespeare was a famous and successful playwright) and law (Shakespeare's plays are full of legal terms. In 1790, English scholar Edmund Malone suggested that the playwright gained this knowledge working in a legal office. In fact, Shakespeare was involved in several legal cases, which may explain his understanding of law).

Chapter 3

Life as Playwright and Actor

William Shakespeare could not just have fun by watching plays in London. He needed to earn a living. His initial jobs in the theatre probably had very little to do with acting or playwriting. A popular story goes that theatre-goers needed someone to tend their horses. William took care of horses and was found so good at the job that he soon began to hire boys to help him. Whether this story is true or not, for hundreds of years, boys who held this job were known as "Shakespeare's boys". William may also have sold theatre tickets or he may have been a prompter's assistant, helping actors with their lines during rehearsals.

Shakespeare possibly learned to write by watching and acting in plays like Thomas Kyd's *The Spanish Tragedy*. Kyd (1558-1594) invented a new type of play called "revenge tragedy" wherein a murder is committed and then violently avenged. One of Shakespeare's first plays was the blood-thirsty revenge tragedy, *Titus Andronicus*. It is not really known when Shakespeare began writing but contemporary allusions and records of performances show that several of his plays were on the London stage by 1592.

He was probably well known by then to be attacked by playwright Robert Greene, who said: "...there is an upstart Crow, beautified with our feathers, that which his Tiger's heart wrapped in a woman's hide, supposes he is as well able to bombast out a blank verse as the best of you and being an absolute Johannes factotum, is in his own conceit the only Shakes-scene in a country."

Though scholars differ on the exact meaning of these words, most agree that Greene was accusing Shakespeare of reaching above his rank in trying to match university-educated writers, nick-named the "University Wits". The group, in the 1590s, included Christopher Marlowe, Thomas Nashe and Robert Greene himself. The phrase parodying the line, "Oh, Tiger's heart wrapped in a woman's hide" from Shakespeare's *Henry VII*, Part 3, along with the pun "Shake-scene" identifies Shakespeare as Greene's target. They wrote plays in unrhymed lines of ten syllables called blank verse, like Marlowe's "Is this the face that launched a thousand ships?" Marlowe's influence can be seen in the opening line of Shakespeare's early play *Henry VI,* Part One, "Hung be the heavens with black, yield day to night!"

Blank verse does not rhyme but it has rhythm. When you clap out a beat or play the drums, you create a rhythm. The rhythm or pattern of most blank verses has a fancy name—the iambic pentameter. If you were to clap your hands to this rhythm, every other beat would be loud, like da-dum, da-dum, da-dum, da-dum, da-dum. This pattern is repeated five times in each line of blank verse. Shakespeare used iambic pentameter to make his words flow as gracefully as notes of music.

Shakespeare's play *Pericles* is set in the Mediterranean with shipwrecks and pirates featuring in the action. Pericles, Prince of Tyre, buries his wife Thaisa at sea after she dies giving birth to their daughter. Thaisa is washed ashore at Ephesus, where she is brought back to life by the miraculous healing power of music.

The Tempest tells the story of a magician called Prospero, the rightful Duke of Milan. He is overthrown by his brother and goes to live on an island with his daughter, his fairy-helper Ariel and a band of other spirits. He uses magic to cause a shipwreck that brings his enemies to the island for punishment.

From 1599 to 1608 was a period of extraordinary literary activity for Shakespeare. During these years, he wrote several comedies and almost all the tragedies that have made him famous. Shakespeare's masterpieces during this period include the comedies *Much Ado about Nothing* and *Twelfth Night*; the history *Henry V*; and the tragedies *Antony and Cleopatra, Hamlet, Julius Caesar, King Lear, Macbeth* and *Othello*.

In 1623, John Hemminges and Henry Condell, two of Shakespeare's friends from the King's Men, published the leather-bound *First Folio*, a collected edition of Shakespeare's plays. It contained thirty-six texts, including eighteen printed for the first time. A folio, from the Latin word for "leaf", is a large book with pages made up of standard sheets, or leaves, of paper folded in half. Hemminges and Condell wrote that their aim was "only to keep the memory of so worthy a friend, and fellow alive, as was our Shakespeare."

First Folio

Many of the plays had already appeared in quarto versions—flimsy books made from sheets of paper folded twice to make four leaves. No evidence suggests that Shakespeare approved these editions, which the *First Folio* describes as "stol'n and surreptitious copies". Alfred Pollard termed some of them "bad quartos" because of their adapted, paraphrased or garbled text, which may have been reconstructed from memory. Where several versions of a play survive, each differs from the other. The differences may stem from copying or printing errors, from notes by actors or audience members, or from Shakespeare's own papers. In some cases, for example, in *Hamlet, Troilus and Cressida* and *Othello*, Shakespeare could have revised the texts between the quarto and folio editions. The folio version of *King Lear* is so different from the 1608 quarto that the *Oxford Shakespeare* printed them both, since these could not be conflated without confusion.

Career in Theatre

Sometime after reaching London, Shakespeare possibly joined one of the city's repertory theatre companies. These companies had on their payroll permanent actors who provided a variety of plays, week after week. These theatre companies were commercial organisations surviving on the admission tickets for their income. Further, they staged plays which the Londoners enjoyed and attended.

There is some indication that Shakespeare had become well known in London theatrical life by 1592. Indeed, Shakespeare was one of the few Elizabethan writers who concentrated almost solely on the theatre as a career. That year, a pamphlet appeared with an apparent reference to Shakespeare. This reference suggested he had become both an actor and a playwright. By 1592, Shakespeare was also an established playwright. Though not having studied in a university, Shakespeare's success was partly because he was a mere player—he knew what worked on stage and what did not. Though no one knows which theatre company Shakespeare had joined before 1594, he was a stockholder in the company called the Lord Chamberlain's Men in 1594. A record is present of payment to Shakespeare and his fellow actors for performance by the company at Queen Elizabeth's court.

Shakespeare appears to have remained an actor throughout his professional life for he was listed as an actor in documents in 1592, 1598, 1603 and 1608, which is to say that at every phase of his career. It could not have been easy to be an actor as well as playwright, but it undoubtedly allowed him much greater control than had he simply surrendered a script to others, as most playwrights did. According to tradition, Shakespeare specialised in good but fairly undemanding roles in his own plays. The ghost in *Hamlet* is the part to which he is most often linked. It would not be wrong to assume the above, given the demands of his not only as writer of the plays but also in all likelihood as the person most closely involved with their staging. Or it could be that he truly enjoyed acting and craved large parts when not distracted by writing of scripts. He was listed as a principal performer in Ben Jonson's *Every Man in His Humour* in 1598 and *Sejanus* in 1603.

By 1594, at least six of Shakespeare's plays had been produced. Between 1529 and 1594, players kept the London theatres closed most of the time. On joining the Lord Chamberlain's Men, he wrote about two plays a year for them and also worked as an actor. The company performed at Theatre in north London, which was owned by James Burbage. His son Richard was the star actor and

Richard Burbage

Cuthbert, another of his sons, managed the business. Richard Burbage was Shakespeare's friend and the greatest tragic actor of his day.

By 1596, Shakespeare had moved to the parish of St. Helen's Bishopsgate and by 1598, he appeared at the top of the list of actors in *Every Man in His Humour*, written by Ben Jonson, a fellow playwright. He is also listed among the actors in Jonson's *Sejanus: His Fall* and he wrote this about Shakespeare, "Whatever he penned, he never blotted out a line." Jonson, a slow and careful writer, considered

Ben Jonson

Shakespeare's ease and speed to be a sign of carelessness. Shakespeare's name on the title pages of his plays presumably became a selling point. Sometime between 1596 and 1599, he moved across River Thames to a district called Bankside, where two theatres—the Rose and the Swan—were built by Philip Henslowe, who was

James Burbage's chief competitor in London as a theatre manager. The Burbages also moved to this district in 1598 and built the famous Globe Theatre. Shakespeare was associated with Globe Theatre for the rest of his active life. He owned shares in it, which brought him much money.

Through the years, the facts of Shakespeare's life have been confused with many tales based on hearsay and legend. During the 1800s in particular, admiration for Shakespeare grew so intense that it resulted in a totally uncritical attitude towards the man and his works. This attitude made Shakespeare almost into a God. However, Shakespeare's reputation was largely that of a popular playwright, not of a writer of unequalled genius. Few people gave him the praise that the later generations heaped on him, with the exception of the English clergyman and schoolmaster Francis Meres. In 1598 Meres wrote *Palladis Tamia: Wit's Treasury*, a book that has become an important source of information about Shakespeare's career. In this book, Meres said of Shakespeare: "As Plautus and Seneca are accounted the best for comedy and tragedy among the Latin, so Shakespeare among the English is the most excellent in both kinds for the stage." Although Meres's praise did not represent everyone's opinion, it indicated that Shakespeare had become an established writer by at least the late 1590s. And he had not yet written most of his great tragedies, such as *Hamlet, Othello, King Lear* and *Macbeth*. His late plays, often known as the romances, date from 1608 onwards and include *The Tempest*.

In 1596, Shakespeare applied for a coat of arms. Despite a lack of proof, he was granted his request. After getting his coat of arms, Shakespeare could write "Gentleman" after his name. This meant much to him, for in his day, actors were classed legally with criminals and vagrants. Later in 1599, he applied for his mother's coat of arms to be added to his own.

Criticism by Anti-Stratfordians

Some people believed that an actor from Stratford-upon-Avon could not have written the plays. Shakespeare's commonplace country background did not fit their image of the genius who wrote the plays. These people, called anti-Stratfordians, proposed several other Elizabethan writers as the authors of Shakespeare's works. The writers they suggested are sometimes called "claimants". Almost all the claimants were members of the nobility or upper class. The anti-Stratfordians believed that only an educated, sophisticated man of high social standing could have written the plays. Sir Francis Bacon was the first and, for many years, the most popular candidate proposed as the real author of Shakespeare's plays. Bacon's followers remain active today. But other anti-Stratfordians have had their own favourites. Edward de Vere, the seventeenth Earl of Oxford, is now more popular than Bacon. Other men to whom authorship has been credited include Roger Manners, the fifth Earl of Rutland; William Stanley, the sixth Earl of Derby and Sir Walter Raleigh. Some anti-Stratfordians have also claimed that the writer Christopher Marlowe was the actual author.

In spite of the claims made for these men, no important Shakespearean scholar doubts that Shakespeare wrote the plays and poems.

Chapter 4

His First Poems

From mid 1592 to 1594, London authorities often closed the public theatres because of repeated outbreaks of plague. The need for new plays thus declined. At this time, Shakespeare began to write poems. The Elizabethans considered the writing of poetry much more important than the writing of plays. Shakespeare perhaps believed that by writing poems he might be able to win the praise that mere playwriting never received.

It wasn't as though Shakespeare didn't have some experience in the field of writing of poetry. Much of the dialogue for his plays had been written in verse form. So far, he had considered himself a dramatist and in terms of reputation, that wasn't necessarily such a great thing to be. Though considered moneymakers, playwrights weren't revered as artists. They were more like hacks, paid to produce on demand, and pretty close to the bottom of the social strata. Poets, on the other hand, were respected members of the society. What they lacked in money power, they made up for in intellectual superiority or so the Elizabethans thought.

In 1593, Shakespeare's long poem *Venus and Adonis* was printed by Richard Field, a Stratford neighbour who had become a London printer. This first poem of Shakespeare was entered in the Stationers' Registrar on April 18th, 1593. Shakespeare dedicated the poem to nineteen-year old Henry Wriothesley, the Earl of Southampton. The poet may have

Henry Wriothesley

believed that the dedication would win him the Earl's favour and support. *Venus and Adonis* quickly became a success.

Field printed Shakespeare's next long poem, *The Rape of Lucrece*, in 1594. In this poem, the virtuous wife Lucrece is raped by the lustful Tarquin. Shakespeare also dedicated this poem to the Earl of Southampton. The wording of the dedication suggests the possibility that the young nobleman had rewarded the author, probably financially, for his dedication in *Venus and Adonis*. Influenced by Ovid's *Metamorphoses*, the poems show the guilt and moral confusion that result from uncontrolled lust. Both proved popular and went through many editions during Shakespeare's lifetime.

A third narrative poem, *A Lover's Complaint*, in which a young woman laments her seduction by a persuasive suitor, was printed in the first edition of the *Sonnets* in 1609. Most scholars now accept that Shakespeare wrote *A Lover's Complaint*. Critics consider that its fine qualities are marred by leaden effects. *The Phoenix and the Turtle*, printed in Robert Chester's *1601 Love's Martyr*, mourns the deaths of the legendary Phoenix and his lover, the faithful turtle dove. In 1599, two early drafts of sonnets 138 and 144 appeared in *The Passionate Pilgrim*, a book of twenty poems published under Shakespeare's name but without his permission. However, the book contained only two of Shakespeare's sonnets and three poems from his comedy *Love's Labour's Lost*. The printer named William Jaggard used Shakespeare's name on the title page to promote the book's sale, which illustrates the playwright's popularity at that time. It is considered unlikely that William wanted any of his deeply personal poems to be revealed to the outside world. But their success did not lead Shakespeare to give up playwriting.

Chapter 5

Theatre Companies

The drama companies consisted of only men and boys because women did not perform on the Elizabethan stage. A typical acting company had eight to twelve sharers, a number of salaried workers and apprentices. The sharers were the company's leading actors as well as its stockholders. They had charge of the company's business activities. They bought plays and costumes, rented theatres, paid fees and split the profits. The salaried workers, who were called hirelings, took minor roles in the plays, performed to music, served as prompters and did various odd jobs. The apprentices were boys who played the roles of women and children.

The acting companies operated under the sponsorship either of a member of the royal family or of an important nobleman. Most sponsorships were in name only and did not include financial support. From 1594 to 1603, Shakespeare's company was sponsored, in turn, by the first and second Lord Hunsdon, a father and son. The first Lord Hunsdon held the important court position of Lord Chamberlain until he died in 1596. In 1597, his son became Lord Chamberlain. Thus, from 1594 to 1603, Shakespeare's company was mostly known as the Lord Chamberlain's Men. After James I became King of England in 1603, he singled out the company for royal favour. It was then known as the King's Men.

Shakespeare was unusual among Elizabethan playwrights. He not only wrote exclusively for his own company but also served as an actor and sharer in it. The close association between Shakespeare, his fellow actors, and the conditions of production had enormous influence on his drama. Shakespeare wrote most of his plays with a particular theatre building in mind and for performers he had frequently acted with. Each major actor in the company specialised in a certain type of role. For example, one played the leading tragic characters and the other the main comic characters; still another played old men. Shakespeare wrote his plays to suit the talents of specific performers. He knew when he created a *Hamlet*, *Othello*, or *King Lear* that the character would be interpreted by Richard Burbage, the company's leading tragic actor.

It is not clear for which companies Shakespeare wrote his early plays. The title page of the 1594 edition of *Titus Andronicus* reveals that the play had been acted by three different troupes. After the plague of 1592-3, Shakespeare's plays were performed by his own company at the Theatre and Curtain in Shoreditch, north of the Thames. Londoners flocked to see the first part of *Henry IV*, in which Leonard Digges records, "Let but Falstaff come, Hal Poins, the rest…and you scarce shall have a room." When the company found themselves in dispute with their landlord, they pulled the Theatre down and used the timbers to construct the Globe Theatre, the first playhouse built by actors for actors.

The Globe Theatre

In 1598, the Globe came into the world one winter night thanks to equal measures of grit and chutzpah. A year earlier the Burbage boys had inherited their father's famous playhouse. Somehow through mismanagement or plain ill luck, the Burbage boys lost the Theatre's land lease. Just before Christmas in 1597, William and the troupe had gathered at the empty theatre. The land wasn't theirs, but the building was—every last board and nail of it! The building in any case was slated for demolition and rather than risk that, they concocted a daring scheme. Richard Burbage enlisted a carpenter and several of his actor friends to dismantle the Theatre in the dead of the night, then carry the timbers across the frozen Thames to Bankside, which had become London's thriving theatre district. There, in the next few months, they assembled a new building from those timbers. When the work was finished eight months later, the Burbages christened their new creation the Globe. The Globe was, in its days, the finest theatre that London had ever seen.

The Globe Theatre

The stage was framed with rich hangings and held up by giant wooden pillars painted to look like marble. The *heaven* or top level of the stage, was decorated with angels and clouds. A trapdoor on the main level of the stage allowed actors to appear and disappear, as if by magic. On the play days, different coloured flags flapped merrily in the breeze. A black flag announced a tragedy, white a comedy and red a history play.

That very year, the Globe opened with Shakespeare and his six associates becoming owners of the Globe, one of the largest theatres in the London area. It may have held as many as 3,000 spectators. The Globe opened in autumn 1599, with *Julius Caesar*, one of the first plays staged. Most of Shakespeare's greatest post-1599 plays were written for the Globe, including *Hamlet, Othello* and *King Lear*.

In 1601, there was a plot to overthrow Queen Elizabeth of England, who had never married. There were rumours of the aging queen having an affair with the handsome young Earl of Essex. In 1601, the Earl of Essex planned a coup to become a king himself. What is highly astonishing is that just before the coup, he asked the Chamberlain's Men to perform *Richard II*, the story of a weak king forced to give up his throne. He tried to ridicule the king in front of the 3,000 people watching the rebellion. He wanted to stir up the audience against Queen Elizabeth. However, she uncovered the plot and threw the Earl into prison before getting him executed.

Now William and the Chamberlain's Men were questioned about their role in the plot. Their answers must have sounded convincing for they were packed up home without being punished. But the event showed how dangerous putting up a play could be!

The King's Men

While *Hamlet's* dark theme made it a difficult play to watch, though it was a big hit and *Othello* thrilled the audience, Queen Elizabeth's failing health gave way and she died in February 1603, without naming the next ruler. Her cousin James, who was the King of Scotland became James I of England on July 25th, 1603. James was a great theatre-lover. He became the patron of Shakespeare's company. As the king, one of his first acts was to change the name of the Chamber-lain's Men to King's Men. To please the king, Shakespeare wrote *Macbeth*, a tragedy with a Scottish setting.

James I of England

The Lord Chamberlain's Men was one of the most popular acting companies in London. Shakespeare was a leading member of the group for the rest of his career. The company took its name from its aristocratic sponsor, the Lord Chamberlain. The group became popular enough that after the death of Elizabeth I and the coronation of James I (1602), the new monarch adopted the company and it became known as the King's Men. Shakespeare's writing shows him to indeed be an actor with many phrases, words and references to acting, but there isn't an academic approach to the art of theatre that might be expected.

King James's support came at a convenient time. An outbreak of plague in 1603 had closed the theatres for long periods, making theatrical life uncertain. In fact, James's entry into London as king had to be postponed until 1604 because of the plague. The King's Men were issued a royal licence and performed seven of Shakespeare's plays at court between November 1st, 1604 and October 31st, 1605, including two performances of the *The Merchant of Venice*.

The King's Men achieved unequalled success and became London's leading theatrical group. In 1608, the company leased the Blackfriars Theatre for twenty-one years and this indoor theatre stood in this heavily populated London district. The Theatre had artificial lighting, was probably heated and served as the company's winter playhouse. Though smaller than the Globe, the entrance charges were higher. The new audience, made up of courtiers and other wealthy Londoners, inspired a new style of playwriting.

The King's Men performed at the Globe during the summer. The indoor setting, combined with the Jacobean fashion for lavishly staged masques, allowed Shakespeare to introduce more elaborate stage devices. In *Cymbeline*, for example, Jupiter descends "in thunder and lightning, sitting upon an eagle; he throws a thunderbolt. The ghosts fall on their knees."

The actors in Shakespeare's company included not only the famous Richard Burbage, but William Kempe, Henry Condell and John Hemminges. Burbage played the leading role in the first performances of many of Shakespeare's plays, including *Richard III*,

Hamlet, Othello and *King Lear*. The popular comic actor, William Kempe, played the servant Peter in *Romeo and Juliet* and Dogberry in *Much Ado About Nothing*, among other characters. He was replaced around the turn of the 16th century by Robert Armin, who played roles such as Touchstone in *As You Like It* and the fool in *King Lear*.

On June 29th, 1613, however, a cannonball was fired on the stage of the Globe during a performance of *Henry VIII*. Sparks lit the thatched roof of the theatre. The structure was engulfed in flames. While the birth of the Globe Theatre, which began with the dismantling of the Theatre, took place under the cover of darkness, the death of the Globe was anything but secretive. The original Globe went out in a true blaze of glory. The audience was apparently so caught up in the action on stage of the play *Henry VIII* that no one noticed the smoke. By the time they did, the building was beyond saving. No one was hurt, but the theatre was burned to the ground. It was not, however, beyond reconstructing—twice. A second Globe Theatre was built on the same site a year later, but it was demolished along with rest of London's Elizabethan theatres around 1644, following the Puritan Revolution. However, a third Globe Theatre, reconstructed in the mid 1990s to replicate the original, now offers regular performances of Shakespeare's plays in a period setting.

Chapter 6

A Head for Business

None can say for certain exactly how Shakespeare worked on a day-to-day basis but it is known that at the height of his career, he wrote an average of two plays per year, which, considering the complexity of his themes and plots, was a pretty good pace. We know that during this same time he earned approximately 200 pounds a year from his writing, quite respectable at that time and significantly better than most of his contemporaries.

As for the myth that the creative types we have come to admire over the years have rarely been good with figures, they were barely able to support themselves and their family and any money they made from their art was allowed to slip through their fingers. In an era when the majority of the theatre folk spent the bulk of their free time in taverns, Shakespeare was the consummate professional and an exception. He was a writer who recognised a good investment when he saw one. A writer in those days had to be smart as well as creative. So while Shakespeare wrote about royalty and politics, he was always careful to couch his opinions in mainstream language and themes. Before any play could go into production, it had to pass muster with the royal censors; Shakespeare's work always did.

At the height of his career he reportedly earned about 200 pounds per year from his writing, a considerably better than average living in turn of the 17th-century England, where a working man's family survived on about 5 pounds per year, but writing was not the only source of Shakespeare's income. He also earned money, maybe as much as 150 pounds a year, as a shareholder in his acting companies. He was apparently relentless about collecting debts owed to him. His name shows up on several tax registers and court documents related to financial disputes. What profits he made went into land and buildings, so that throughout his life he amassed enough money to live out his last years quite comfortably on his estate in Stratford.

In 1597, William purchased the New Place, which was one of the most prominent and desired properties in all of Stratford.

Shakespeare's swanky home in New Place was the second largest house in Stratford. It had once belonged to Sir Hugh Clopton, one of the town's most prominent citizens and a former Lord Mayor of London. Drawings of the period depict New Place as having three storeys and five gables. It was warmed by more than ten fireplaces, which meant there were probably many more rooms; fireplaces in those times were taxable and thus would have been kept to a minimum. The extensive grounds included formal gardens, two orchards, a chapel, two barns and servants' quarters. That Shakespeare could afford to live in such luxury was indicative of the financial success he attained from a lifetime of work. It was also quite a step up from his birthplace, a few blocks away on Henley Street.

This was his greatest financial gain made with an investment of some 440 pounds. This property doubled in value and earned him sixty pounds as income each year. Some academics speculate that this investment gave the Bard the time he needed to write plays uninterrupted and we know that he was indeed thought of as a businessman in the Stratford area. Further, given his father's known financial hardship from 1576, William must either have used his own money to buy this expensive property or the father might have placed money in his son's name. It is also quite possible William might have bought this prominent property with money from his plays. It is estimated that roughly fifteen of his thirty-seven plays would have been written and performed by 1597.

Interestingly, some say that in 1601, he had bought roughly 107 acres of arable land with twenty acres of pasturage for twenty pounds in Old Stratford. Yet, another record confirms that John Comb's will bequeathed to the Bard the princely sum of just five pounds, making him into a rich man.

In March 1613, Shakespeare bought a gatehouse in the Blackfriars priory and from November 1614 onwards he was in London for weeks with his son-in-law, John Hall.

Chapter 7

Sonnets

People have always wanted to know more about Shakespeare's private life. They have searched his plays for hints, with little result. In 1609, a London publisher named Thomas Thorpe published a book called *Shakespeare's Sonnets*. The volume contained more than 154 sonnets that Shakespeare had written over the years. Scholars are not certain when each of the 154 sonnets was composed, but evidence suggests that Shakespeare wrote sonnets throughout his career for a private readership. Even before the two unauthorised sonnets appeared in *The Passionate Pilgrim* in 1599, Francis Meres had referred in 1598 to Shakespeare's "surged sonnets among his private friends." Few analysts believe that the published collection follows Shakespeare's intended sequence. He seems to have planned two contrasting series, one about uncontrollable lust for a married woman of dark complexion (the "dark lady"), and the other about conflicted love for a fair young man (the "fair youth"). It remains unclear if these figures represent real individuals, or if the authorial "I" who addresses them represents Shakespeare himself, though Wordsworth believed that with the sonnets, "Shakespeare unlocked his heart." The 1609 edition was dedicated to a "Mr. W.H.", credited as "the only begetter" of the poems. It is not known whether this was written by Shakespeare himself or by the publisher, Thomas Thorpe, whose initials appear at the foot of the dedication page. Critics praise the *Sonnets* as profound meditation on the nature of love, sexual passion, procreation, death and time.

Scholars have long been specially curious about the dedication Thorpe wrote to the book. The dedication reads, in modernised spelling: "To the only begetter of these ensuing sonnets, Mr. W.H." Generations of researchers have failed to identify Mr. W.H. Scholars have also analysed the sonnets to determine to what extent they are autobiographical. But their analyses have proved contradictory and generally unsatisfactory. Many critics suggest that readers simply enjoy the sonnets as some of the finest verses in English literature, instead of examining the poems as autobiographical statements.

Chapter 8

Style of Presentation

During the reign of Queen Elizabeth, "drama became the ideal means to capture and convey the diverse interests of the time." Stories of various genres were enacted for audiences consisting of both the wealthy and educated and the poor and illiterate. Shakespeare served his dramatic apprenticeship at the height of the Elizabethan period, in the years following the defeat of the Spanish Armada; he retired at the height of the Jacobean period, not long before the start of the thirty years' war. His verse style, his choice of subjects, and his stagecraft all bear the marks of both the periods. His style changed not only in accordance with his own tastes and developing mastery, but also in accord with the tastes of the audiences for whom he wrote.

Shakespeare's first plays were written in the conventional style of the day. He wrote them in a stylised language that does not always spring naturally from the needs of the characters or the drama. The poetry depends on extended, sometimes elaborate metaphors and conceits, and the language is often rhetorical— written for actors to declaim rather than speak. The grand speeches in *Titus Andronicus*, in the view of some critics, often hold up the action, for example, and the verse in *Two Gentlemen of Verona* has been described as stilted.

Soliloquy

Soon, however, Shakespeare began to adapt the traditional styles for his own purposes. His plays became notable for their use of soliloquies, in which a character makes a speech to himself or herself, so the audience can understand the character's inner motivations and conflicts. Among his most famous soliloquies is when the tragic hero Hamlet feels so hopeless that he considers killing himself. He says, "To be, or not to be: that is the question…" In other words, he is wondering whether "to live or to die". He could not make up his mind about that! The other soliloquies are "All the world's a stage…", "Tomorrow and tomorrow and tomorrow…", and "What a piece of work is a man…".

The opening soliloquy of *Richard III* has its roots in the self-declaration of vice in medieval drama. At the same time, Richard's vivid self-awareness looks forward to the soliloquies of Shakespeare's mature plays. No single play marks a change from the traditional to the freer style. Shakespeare combined the two throughout his career, with *Romeo and Juliet* perhaps the best example of mixing of the styles. By the time *Romeo and Juliet*, *Richard II* and *A Midsummer Night's Dream* came in the mid 1590s, Shakespeare had begun to write a more natural poetry. He increasingly tuned his metaphors and images to the needs of the drama itself.

Shakespeare's standard poetic form was blank verse which was usually unrhymed and consisted of ten syllables to a line, spoken with a stress on every second syllable. The blank verse of his early plays is quite different from that of his late ones. It is often beautiful, but its sentences end to start, pause and finish at the end of the lines, with the risk of monotony. Once Shakespeare mastered traditional blank verse, he began to interrupt and vary its flow. This technique releases the new power and flexibility of the poetry in plays such as *Julius Caesar* and *Hamlet*. Shakespeare uses it, for example, to convey the turmoil in Hamlet's mind.

> *"Sir, in my heart there was a kind of fighting*
> *that would not let me sleep. Methought I lay*
> *worse than the mutinies in the bilboes. Rashly—*
> *and prais'd be rashness for it—let us know*
> *our indiscretion sometimes serves us well…"*

After *Hamlet*, Shakespeare varied his poetic style further, particularly in the more emotional passages of the late tragedies. The literary critic A.C. Bradley described this style as "more concentrated, rapid, varied, and, in construction, less regular, not seldom twisted or elliptical." In the last phase of his career, Shakespeare adopted many techniques as to achieve these effects. These included run-on lines, irregular pauses and stops, and extreme variations in sentence structure and length. In *Macbeth*, for example, the language darts from one unrelated metaphor or simile to another:

> *"…was the hope drunk*
> *wherein you dressed yourself?"*

"...pity, like a naked newborn babe
striding the blast, or heaven's cherubim, hors'd
upon the sightless scouriers of the air..."

The listener is challenged to complete the sense. The late romances, with their shifts in time and surprising turns of plot, inspired a last poetic style in which long and short sentences are set against one another, clauses are piled up, subject and object are reversed, as words are omitted, creating an effect of spontaneity.

Shakespeare's poetic genius was allied with a practical sense of the theatre. Like all playwrights of the time, Shakespeare dramatised stories from sources such a Petrarch and Holinshed. He reshaped each plot to create several centres of interest and show as many sides of a narrative to the audience as possible. This strength of design ensures that a Shakespeare play can survive translation, cutting across wide interpretation without loss to its core drama. As Shakespeare's mastery grew, he gave his characters clearer and more varied motivations and distinctive patterns of speech.

Shakespeare preserved aspects of his earlier style in the later plays, however. His last three plays were collaborations, probably with John Fletcher, who succeeded him as the house playwright for the King's Men. In his late romances, he deliberately returned to a more artificial style, which emphasised the illusion of theatre.

To end many scenes in his plays, he used a rhyming couplet for suspense. A typical example is provided in *Macbeth*. As Macbeth leaves the stage to murder Duncan (to the sound of a chiming clock), he says,

> *"Hear it not Duncan, for it is a knell*
> *that summons thee to heaven or to hell."*

Shakespeare's writing (especially in his plays) also features extensive word play in which double entendes and clever rhetorical flourishes are repeatedly used. Humour is a key element in all of Shakespeare's plays. Although a large amount of his comical talent is evident in his comedies, some of the most entertaining scenes and characters are found in tragedies, such as *Hamlet* and histories, such as *Henry IV*, Part I. Shakespeare's humour was largely influenced by Plautus.

Chapter 9

Last Years of Life

In 1607, when Shakespeare was-forty three, he may have suffered a serious physical breakdown. About this time, Shakespeare became one of the groups of now-famous writers who gathered at the Mermaid Tavern located on Bread Street in Cheapside. The Friday Street Club (also called the Mermaid Club) was formed by Sir Walter Raleigh. Ben Jonson was its leading spirit and Shakespeare was a popular member. He was admired for his talent and loved for his kindliness.

Thomas Fuller, writing about fifty years later, gave an amusing account of the conversational duels between Shakespeare and Jonson: "Many were the wit-combats betwixt him and Ben Jonson, which two I behold like a Spanish great galleon and an English man-of-war. Master Jonson (like the former) was built far higher in learning; solid, but slow, in his performances. Shakespeare, with the English man-of-war, lesser in bulk, but lighter in sailing, could turn with all tides, tack about, and take advantage of all winds, by the quickness of his wit and invention."

Jonson sometimes criticised Shakespeare harshly. Nevertheless he later wrote a eulogy of Shakespeare that is remarkable for its feeling and acuteness. In it he said:

> *"Leave thee alone, for the comparison*
> *of all that insolent Greece or haughty Rome*
> *sent forth, or since did from their ashes come.*
> *Triumph, my Britain, thou hast one to show*
> *to whom all scenes of Europe homage owe.*
> *He was not of an age, but for all time!"*

After 1606-1607, Shakespeare wrote fewer plays and none are attributed to him after 1613. After finishing work on *The Tempest* in 1611, Shakespeare returned to live in Stratford. Although he had inherited the house in Henley Street when his father died, he went to live in New Place, which he had bought for his family in 1597. The playwright enjoyed only a few years of retirement. Maybe he puttered a little in one of his gardens or spent time bouncing his granddaughter Elizabeth on his knee. It is known that he remained active in real-estate transactions. A surviving 1614 document, concerning a controversy over the enclosure of some common land in which he had a share, bears his name.

On February 10th, 1616, Shakespeare would have probably attended his daughter Judith's wedding to Thomas Quiney, a tavern-keeper, two months before his death. Quiney was charged in the local church court with "fornication". A woman named Margaret Wheeler had given birth to a child and claimed it was Quiney's; she and the child however died soon after. Quiney was thereafter disgraced and Shakespeare revised his will to ensure that Judith's interest in his estate was protected from possible mal-feasance on Quiney's part. Thus Shakespeare left the bulk of his large estate to his elder daughter Susanna. Susanna had married a physician John Hall in 1607. The terms instructed that she pass it down intact to the "first son of her body".

The Quineys had three children, all of whom died without marrying. The Halls had one child, Elizabeth, who married twice but died without children in 1670, ending Shakespeare's direct line. Shakespeare's daughter Susanna went to live at Hall Croft in Stratford with her new husband John Hall. Shakespeare approved of the match and would have returned to Stratford for the wedding. During his last years while working in London, Shakespeare returned to Stratford with increasing regularity. He probably attended most family events, such as his mother's funeral in 1608, and his granddaughter Elizabeth's christening in the same year.

It seems he simply faded away, a rather pedestrian end for a poet and playwright whose work we are still reading centuries later. Supposedly Shakespeare died on his birthday, if the tradition that he was born on April 23rd is correct.

Shakespeare died on April 23rd, 1616, apparently from an infection contracted by consuming spoiled herring, at the age of fifty-two. Some say it occurred following a dinner with Ben Jonson and some other theatre friends, where he drank a little too much wine. Nobody knows about the state of his health but it is known that on March 25th, 1616, he summoned his lawyer and made changes to his will. In the text of the document he described himself as being "in perfect health & memorie, God be praysed."

William Shakespeare made the changes to his will, in which his signatures are shaky and the will bears certain signs of confusion; he could not evidently recall the names of his brother-in-law Tomas Hart or one of Hart's sons, though it is equally odd that none of the five witnesses supplied these details either.

Much has been read into the bequest Shakespeare famously made in his will, leaving his wife Anne, who was probably entitled to one-third of his estate automatically, "my second best bed", leading to much speculation. Some scholars see the bequest as an insult to Anne, whereas others believe that the second-best bed would have been the matrimonial bed and therefore rich in

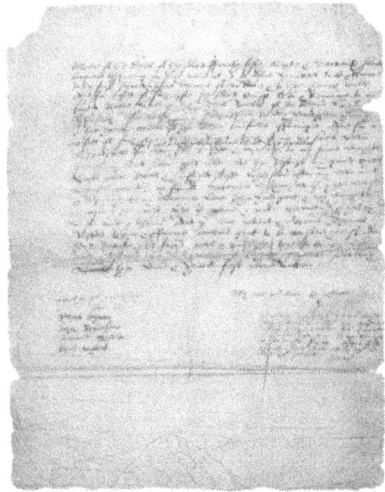

Will's will

significance. However, in Elizabethan custom, the best bed in the house was reserved for guests. Therefore, the bed that Shakespeare bequeathed to Anne could have been their marital bed and thus significant. The logical conclusion however would be that Shakespeare, the last surviving of his brothers, was an old man for his times and Anne being eight years older than him, may well have been feeble and dependent on her daughters. He would not have expected her to outlive him by any great length of time and thus it made sense to leave the estate directly to the daughters.

Shakespeare was buried in the chancel of the Holy Trinity Church in Stratford-upon-Avon, two days after his death. He was granted the honour of burial in the chancel not on account of his fame as a playwright but for purchasing a share of the tithe of the church for 440 pounds, a considerable amount of money at that time. Sometime before 1623, a stone monument was erected in his memory on the north wall of the Holy Trinity Church. The painted statue in the posture of writing is likely to be an accurate portrait of the playwright because it was approved by his family.

Shakespeare's stone monument

The sculptor, Geerart Janssen had a workshop near the Globe and may well have known Shakespeare himself. Each year on his claimed birthday, a new quill pen is placed in the writing hand of the bust. Its plaque compared him to Nestor, Socrates and Virgil. A stone slab covering his grave in inscribed with a curse against moving his bones. He is believed to have written the epitaph on his tombstone. He wrote thus:

> *Good friend, for Jesus' sake forbear,*
> *to dig the dust enclosed here.*
> *Blest be the man that spares these stones,*
> *And cursed be he that moves my bones.*

PART II

Chapter 10

England of Shakespeare's Days

Shakespeare's works reflect the cultural, social and political conditions of the Elizabethan era. Knowledge of these conditions can provide a better understanding of Shakespeare's plays and poems. For instance, most Elizabethans believed in ghosts, witches and magicians. Though no biographical evidence exists that Shakespeare held such beliefs, but he wrote about them very effectively in his plays. Ghosts play an important part in *Hamlet, Julius Caesar, Macbeth* and *Richard III*. Witches are major characters in *Macbeth*; Prospero, the hero of *The Tempest* is a magician. He is overthrown by his bother and goes to live on an island with his daughter, his fairy-helper Ariel and a band of other spirits. He uses magic to cause a shipwreck that brings his enemies to the island for punishment.

No less is the role played by adventures, fairies and the clown or the court jester in Shakespeare's plays. He introduced a new style of play writing between 1608 and 1611, when he wrote four plays for the Blackfriars. Known as the romances, they had common fairytale plots, the adventures of noble heroes and heroines and families broken apart and reunited.

The English renaissance reached its peak in the reign of Queen Elizabeth I (1558-1603). She ruled England for forty-five years. In this period England was emerging from the Middle Ages. It changed from an absorbing interest in heaven and an afterlife to an ardent wonder about this world and man's earthly existence. It was an age when men were curious, active and brave. They boldly explored the past, the Earth and themselves.

Queen Elizabeth I

At its best, the period showed an intellectual and physical daring. It produced such adventurers as Walter Raleigh and Francis Drake. It had such statesmen as Lord Burghley and such scholar-gentlemen as Philip Sidney. Philosophers such as Francis Bacon, scientists such as William Gilbert and poets such as William Shakespeare belonged to this period.

At its worst the age was extravagant and brutal. Its extravagance showed in the general population's dress, manners and speech which were elaborate and ornate. The language was growing fast. It was suited to magnificent poetry. Shakespeare's vocabulary was large, but its size is less remarkable than its expressiveness. English speech reached it peak of strength between 1600 and 1610. Then the King James's version of the Bible was being made, Bacon was writing his famous *Essays* and Shakespeare was composing his great tragedies.

London was the largest city in northern Europe and ten times the size of any other English town during the Elizabethan era. It is supposed to have had nearly 2,00,000 persons in 1600. In the 1580s, London was a bustling, crowded place with narrow dark streets littered with all sorts of rubbish. Unhygienic conditions led to frequent epidemics of plague, in which thousands of people

Plague in London

died. Nobody knew how the plague spread, but when there was an outbreak, it seemed sensible to avoid crowded places.

Elizabethans were keenly aware of death and the brevity of life. They lived in constant fear of plague. When an epidemic struck, they saw victims carted off to common graves.

By law, the city's playhouses could not open if more than thirty people died in one week. Between 1592 and 1594, the plague was so bad that the playhouses had to stay closed for over two years. The companies of actors left London to tour the countryside in order to make a living. There was no demand for Shakespeare to write new plays, so he turned to poetry.

The people of the English middle class were stern, moral and independent. Moralists felt it necessary to preach against the lowering of morals, the oppression of the poor and the greediness of the nobles. London's citizens held fast to their rights. They did not hesitate to defy the royal court if it became too arrogant.

Nobles, citizens and common people, all loved the stage, its pageantry and poetry. Wealthy people encouraged and supported the actors. They paid for the processions, masques and tournaments which the public loved to watch. Men of the royal court competed with one another in dress, entertainment and flattery of the queen.

Most houses in London were overcrowded and the inner rooms dark and musty. A newcomer would have been struck by the noise, the dirt and the smells of the city. The city was full of street sellers shouting out special cries to attract customers. Men and women wandered on the streets, selling everything from vegetables, fish, wine, toys and books to quills and ink, fruit, brooms, pies and second-hand clothes. They competed for custom with the craftsmen and tradesmen working in the shops that lined the noisy, narrow streets.

Crossing London Bridge one could have been shocked by the sight of the heads of executed traitors rotting on poles. He would also have been impressed by the beauty of the grand churches and the riverside mansions of London's wealthy merchants and nobles.

However, it possessed other factors which made it an exciting city. It was the commercial land, banking centre of England and one of the world's chief trading centres. The city was run by wealthy traders known as merchants. The richest merchants served as officials, called aldermen, on a ruling council headed by the Lord Mayor. Trade was central to the prosperity of

Merchant and his wife

the city and every craft and trade had its own controlling organisation called a guild.

The queen and her dazzling court thus lived in the city for much of each year, adding to the colour and excitement. Even before the playhouses appeared on the scene, London had many different forms of entertainment to offer its citizens. The city's importance attracted people like artists, courtiers, teachers, musicians and writers, all flocking to London to seek advancement.

Yet, death and violence also fascinated many Elizabethans. Londoners enjoyed watching cruel blood sports, such as fights between bulls, bears and packs of dogs and often gathered to watch executions. Traitors' heads were displayed on poles on London Bridge to warn the public against committing treason. Many people passed their time by gambling at dice and cards or playing sports, such as bowls. Gambling was a risky pastime because London was full of criminals who made a living by cheating at cards and dice. These cheats were called 'coneycatchers' and they were always on the lookout for newcomers from the countryside like William Shakespeare. They called their victims 'coneys' (rabbits).

Londoners gather to watch an execution

At Bankside, Londoners could see bull-baiting with bulldogs that had been specially bred and trained for sport. The bulldogs were trained to leap at the bull's face and they would hang on to its nose or ears, while the angry bull did its best to shake it off. When Shakespeare came to London, most people were living in the old part of the city on the north side of the River Thames, still surrounded by medieval walls. But London was spreading fast in all directions, swelled by the rising number of incomers. Bankside, on the south bank of the river, was rapidly becoming London's main entertainment centre.

Walking near the River Thames, Shakespeare would have been greeted by the watermen's shouts of "Westward ho!" and "Eastward ho!" as they called out to passengers. The watermen rowed Londoners up and down the river and across to Bankside and back. The Thames was crowded with boats of all sizes, including the gilded royal barge taking Queen Elizabeth to and from her palace at Greenwich.

England, however, was still Merrie England. It had the best inns and the richest and most varied foods in Europe. Its people were the best clothed and housed.

The wide range of knowledge that Shakespeare shows in his plays could have been the kind that could be absorbed by being in the company of informed persons or his deep involvement in London life.

Chapter 11

Drama in Elizabethan Society

Queen Elizabeth had royal palaces around London at Whitehall, Richmond and Greenwich. Her royal barge carried her back and forth along the River Thames. Young male courtiers flattered by comparing her to the Roman Moon Goddess Diana and called her Gloriana, the glorious one. Londoners were fascinated by what Shakespeare called "court news" and as seen in the play *King Lear*, "who loses and who wins, who's in, who's out."

During her reign, the country grew in wealth and power, despite plagues and other calamities. The queen's freedom was no greater than that of all Englishwomen. Like her, they talked, joked and even cursed like men (women do exactly that in Shakespeare's comedies).

Elizabeth was sometimes carried through London by her leading courtiers in a palanquin or a covered litter. The procession gave ordinary people the chance to catch a glimpse of their queen.

Royal procession

The queen was the symbol of the glory of England. To her people, Elizabeth I stood for beauty and greatness.

Elizabeth enjoyed watching plays, although she never visited the public playhouses. Instead, the players were commanded to give private performances for the court in the palaces around London. Before he became a playwright, Shakespeare would have been known to the queen as a player, from court performances.

From 1584 to 1604, Protestant England was at war with Catholic Spain, ruled by King Philip II. The most dangerous moment of war with Spain came in 1588, when Phillip II of Spain sent a huge war fleet called the Armada to invade England. This ended in disaster for Spain. The Armada was beaten in battle and scattered by storms. The English took this as a sign that God was on their side. The war created a mood of patriotism in the country and people wanted to see plays drawn from English history with battles on the stage. So, in the 1590s, Shakespeare wrote nine plays dealing with English history, featuring kings, wars and battles for the throne.

Shakespeare did not have any fancy notions. He listened to what the public said and was quick to detect changes in popular taste. He wrote his plays to be acted, not read. He took whatever forms were attracting attention and made them better. To save time, he borrowed plots and put down other men's thoughts in his own words.

A dramatist in those days was also likely to be an actor and producer. So Shakespeare joined a theatre company and became its playwright. He sold his manuscripts to it and kept no personal rights in them. Revising old plays and working with another writer on new ones were common. Such methods saved time. The demand for plays was great and could never be fully met.

Manuscripts of Shakespeare, with the possible exception of a scene from *Sir Thomas More* and very few manuscripts of other dramatists of the period, have survived. The dramas were written to be played, not printed and were hardly considered literature at all.

A company of players was a cooperative group that shared the profits. Its members had no individual legal or political rights. Instead, the company looked for a patron among the rich nobles. Members became his "servants" or "men" and received his protection. A company was usually made up of eight or ten men who took the main parts. Other actors were hired as needed. Boys took the female roles as women did not appear on the stage.

When Shakespeare came to London, he found the theatre alive and strong. People enjoyed going to the theatre. Plays were shrewdly written for public taste. The theatre was as popular then as movies and television are now. The first public theatre was opened in 1576. A group of talented men, the University Wits, had already developed new types of plays out of old forms and had learned what the public wanted. Playwrights of the time were practical men, bent on making a living. They may have been well educated, but they were more eager to fill the theatres than to please the critics. The result was that almost from the start the drama was a popular art. It was not, as in France, a learned and classical art.

Theatre and Stage in Elizabethan Era

Theatre was changing when Shakespeare first arrived on the scene in the late 1580s or early 1590s. Dramatists writing of London's new commercial playhouses were combining two different strands of dramatic tradition into a new and distinctively Elizabethan synthesis. Earlier the most common forms of popular theatre were the Tudor morality plays. These plays, which blend piety with farce and slapstick, were allegories in which the characters were personified moral attributes, which validated the virtues of godly life by prompting the protagonist to choose such a life over evil. The characters and plot situations were largely symbolic rather than realistic. The other strand of dramatic tradition was classical aesthetic theory derived essentially from Aristotle. This theory came to be better known through its Roman interpreters and practitioners. At the universities academic plays were staged based on Roman closet dramas. These plays, usually performed in Latin, adhered to classical ideas of utility and decorum, but they were also more static, valuing lengthy speeches over physical action.

Performances were further slowed down by the need for frequent pauses to change the scenery, creating a perceived need for even more cuts in order to keep the performance length within tolerable limits. This was most true of Shakespeare's plays which were found too long to be performed without substantial cuts.

Going to the theatre in Shakespeare's days was a completely different experience than it is today. The Globe was typical of those theatres, with a majority of the audience standing in the open air in front of the stage. If it rained, most of the audience would get wet.

> They were not a quiet bunch but a riotous crowd who could pur-
> chase food from strolling vendors during the course of the perfor-
> mance. If the performance failed to please, they would talk, jeer,
> catcall or hiss. For twice the price of admission the middle class
> could sit in seats with a roof over their heard, in curved tiers around
> the inside of the building.

Public theatres were usually round, wooden buildings with
three galleries of seats. The pit, or main floor, had no roof. There
were no seats in the pit and its occupants were called 'groundlings'
because they stood on the ground. Admission to the pit was usually a penny. The galleries, boxes and stage cost more. Plays were
put on in the afternoon.

Private theatres had a large platform for the stage that projected into the pit. This arrangement allowed the audience to watch
from the front and sides. The performers, nearly surrounded by
spectators, thus had close contact with most of their audience.
They were mostly square and entirely roofed. Actors entered and
left the stage through two or more doorways at the back of the
stage. Behind the doorways were retiring (dressing) rooms. At the
rear of the stage, there was a curtained discovery space. Scholars
disagree about the details of this feature, but the space could be
used to 'discover', that is, reveal one or two characters by opening
the curtains. The characters could also hide there or eavesdrop on
conversations among characters up front of the main stage. The
gallery that hung over the back of the main stage served as an upper
stage but could be used as a balcony or the top of a castle wall. The
upper stage allowed Elizabethan dramatists to give their plays

vertical action in addition to the usual horizontal movement. Some theatres may have had a small third-level room for musicians.

A small roof projected over the upper stage and the back part of the main stage. Atop the roof was a hut that contained machinery to produce sound effects and various special effects, such as the lowering of an actor playing a God. The underside of the hut was sometimes called the heavens. Two pillars supported the structure. The underside of the heavens was richly painted and the interior of the theatre undoubtedly had a number of other decorative features.

The main stage had a large trap door. Actors playing the parts of ghosts and spirits could rise and disappear through the door. The trap door, when opened, could also serve as a grave.

Shakespeare wrote most of his plays for the Globe Theatre. Historical research indicates that its main stage was about 40 feet (12 metres) wide and projected 27 feet (8 metres) into the pit and had a roof of its own. Behind it was a recessed inner stage, which could be hidden by curtains. Above the inner stage was a second inner stage, with curtains and a balcony. Above this was a music room. Its front could be used for dramatic action. On top of the stage roof were hoists for raising and lowering actors and properties. On performance days a flag was flown from a turret above the hoists. The outer stage was generally used for outdoor scenes and mass effects. The inner stage was used for indoor scenes and for cozy effects, as between lovers. The upper stage was used for scenes at windows or walls.

The Elizabethans may have used no scenery, but their stage was not entirely bare. They used good-sized properties, heavy hangings and elaborate furniture. Generally the setting was unknown to the audience until the characters identified it with a few lines of dialogue. In addition, the main stage had no curtain. One scene could follow another quickly because there was no curtain to close and open and no scenery to change. The lack of scenery also allowed the action to flow freely from place to place, as in modern motion pictures. The action of Shakespeare's *Antony and Cleopatra*, for example, shifts smoothly and easily back and forth between ancient Egypt and Rome. As a result this play had more than 40 changes of scene.

Although the stage lacked scenery, various props were used, such as thrones, swords, banners, rocks, trees, tables and beds. *Richard III* calls for two tents, one at each end of the stage.

Costumes, Lights and Sound Effects

The absence of scenery did not result in dull or drab productions. Acting companies spent much money on colourful costumes, largely to produce visual splendour. Costume design is critical to the success of modern-day drama but in Shakespeare's time it was the actors who supplied their own apparel. They could pick up whatever was available in the dressing room or purchase special items at their own expense. A variety of periods of design could stand next to one another on

Fashion for the stage

the stage. Their costumes, usually copied from the fashionable clothes of the day, were rich. Flashing swords and swirling banners also added colour and excitement.

All lighting was natural. Plays began at 2 o'clock, the beginning of the show being announced by a trumpet fanfare and three sharp knocks. Night-time could be suggested by the actors carrying torches or lanterns, but again the language was there to support the stage setting. For example, Oberon evoked the night with "I'll meet by moonlight, proud Titania!"

Sound effects had an important part in Elizabethan drama. Trumpet blasts and drum rolls were common. Sometimes unusual sounds were created, such as "the noise of a sea-fight" called for in *Antony and Cleopatra*. In this play, the playwright included mysterious-sounding chords to set the mood before a fatal battle. Music also played a vital role. Shakespeare filled *Twelfth Night* with songs.

Chapter 12

Drama in Shakespeare's Days

Shakespeare reached maturity as a dramatist at the end of Elizabeth's reign and in the first years of the reign of James. In these years, he responded to a deep shift in popular tastes, both in subject matter and approach. At the turn of the decade, he responded to the vogue for dramatic satire initiated by the boy players at Blackfriars and St. Paul's. As the need of the decade, he seems to have attempted to capitalise on the new fashion for tragicomedy, even collaboration with John Fletcher, the writer, who had popularised the genre in England.

The influence of younger dramatists, such as John Marston and Ben Jonson is seen not only in the problem plays, which dramatise intractable human problems of greed and lust, but also in the darker tone of the Jacobean tragedies. The Marlovian, heroic mode of the Elizabethan tragedies is gone, replaced by a darker vision of heroic nature caught in environments of pervasive corruption. As a sharer in both the Globe and in the King's Men, Shakespeare never wrote for the boys' companies; however, his early Jacobean work is markedly influenced by the techniques of the new, satiric dramatists. One play, *Troilus and Cressida* may even have been inspired by the *War of the Theatres*.

Shakespeare's final plays hearken back to his Elizabethan comedies in their use of the romantic situation and incident. In these plays, however, the sombre elements that are largely glossed over in the earlier plays are brought to the fore and often rendered dramatically vivid. This change is related to the success of tragicomedies such as *Philaster*, although uncertainty of dates make the nature and direction of the influence unclear. From the evidence of the title page to the *The Two Noble Kinsmen* and from textual analysis it is believed by some editors that Shakespeare ended his career in collaboration which Fletcher, who succeeded him as house playwright for the King's Men. These last plays resemble Fletcher's tragicomedies in their attempt to find a comic mode capable of dramatising more serious events than had his earlier comedies.

Shakespeare wrote more than 350 years ago, hence a person with no knowledge of literature may find it difficult to enjoy his plays. The language he used is naturally somewhat different from the language of today. Besides, he wrote in verse. Verse permits a free use of words that may not be understood by some readers. His plays are often fanciful. This may not appeal to matter-of-fact people who are used to modern realism. For all these reasons, readers may find him difficult. The worst handicap to enjoyment is the notion that Shakespeare is a "classic", a writer to be approached with awe. The stage had much to do with the form of Shakespeare's plays.

Here it needs to be remembered that Shakespeare wrote his plays for everyday people and that many in the audience were uneducated. They looked upon him as a funny, exciting and loveable entertainer, not as a great poet. People today should read him as the people in his day listened to him. The excitement and enjoyment of the plays will banish most of the difficulties.

In Shakespeare's days, with no women actors, men made up as women seemed natural somehow. With no stage lighting and with the daytime sky above, the author had to write speeches about the time, season and weather of the play. There are more then forty such speeches in *Macbeth*. The actors were close to the audience, the groundlings were close to the aristocrats. Shakespeare had to appeal to them all. So he mixed horseplay with philosophy and coarseness with lovely poetry. Moreover, Shakespeare did borrow themes from novels by Plutarch and Holinshed, but he made changes to suit the theme of his plays and these changes show his genius as a dramatist.

Because the stage was open and free, it permitted quick changes and rapid action. As a result *Antony and Cleopatra* had more than forty changes of scene. The outer stage, projecting into the audience, encouraged speechmaking. This may be the reason for the long and impassioned speeches of the plays.

For the theatre, Shakespeare wrote at least thirty-seven plays. The chief sources of his plots were Plutarch's *Parallel Lives of Illustrious Men*, Raphael Holinshed's *Chronicles of England, Scotland and Ireland* and some Italian novella or short tales. He borrowed a few plays from older dramas and from English stories. What he did with the sources is more important than the sources themselves.

If his original gave him what he needed, he used it closely. If not, he changed it. These changes show his genius as a dramatist.

Shakespeare's Plots and Characters

Shakespeare's knowledge of men and poetic skill combined to make him the greatest of playwrights. His plots alone show that he was a master playwright. He built his plays with care. He seldom wrote a speech that did not forward the action, develop character or help the imagination of the spectator. The plays therefore need to be read twice. The first reading should be a quick one to get the story. The second, more leisurely, reading should bring out the details. The language itself should be studied. It has great expressiveness and concentrated meaning.

Many of Shakespeare's plots are frankly farfetched. He belonged to an age which was romantic and poetic. People still had the power to make believe. They did not go to the theatre to see real life. They wanted to be carried away to other times and places or to a land of fancy. The imaginative reader today loves him for the same reason. There were really no such places as his Bohemia or Illyria or Forest of Arden, though the names were real. He has never been equalled in the invention of supernatural creatures—ghosts, witches and fairies. But his are realistic in the sense that is true to life. His plots as in *King Lear*, *A Midsummer Night's Dream* and *The Tempest* may seem fantastic but they are powerfully and eternally true.

Shakespeare's people are alive and three-dimensional. They live in the mind as warmly as close friends. His best portrayals are those of his great heroes. Yet even his minor characters are almost as good. For example, he created in his plays more than twenty young women, all about the same age, of the same station in life and with the same social background. They are as different, however, as any twenty girls in real life. The same can be said of his old women, men of action, churchmen, kings, villains, dreamers, fools and country people.

Shakespeare's play *Richard II* tells the story of the overthrow of King Richard II by his cousin Henry Bolingbroke, who later became Henry IV. The play contains Shakespeare's most famous patriotic speech spoken by the dying John of Gaunt: "This happy breed of men, this little world, this precious stone set in a silver sea…this blessed plot, this earth, this realm, this England." In *Richard III*, Shakespeare created one of his most famous villains. Richard murders his nephews in order to become king of England. The play ends with his death in a battle at the hands of Henry Tudor, Elizabeth I's grandfather. Henry says, "The day is ours, the bloody dog is dead."

Sir John Falstaff is the drunken old knight who befriends young Prince Hal in Shakespeare's two *Henry IV* plays. The plays show a series of rebellions against Henry IV, whose troubled reign is God's punishment for overthrowing Richard II. Prince Hal grows into a heroic figure who will make a great king, but first he has to reject Falstaff. The same Prince Hal reappears as the king in *Henry V*, the story of England's great victory over the French at the Battle of Agincourt in 1415. "Follow your spirit," cries the king, rallying his men, "and upon this charge, cry God for Harry, England and Saint George!" The central theme of the plays was the need for order.

However, the optimism of the late 1500s faded rapidly. By the time Queen Elizabeth died in 1603, the English were struggling with many social and economic problems. These problems were complicated by minor wars with other countries—wars that often seemed without purpose. To many English persons the world appeared to be deteriorating and becoming, in Hamlet's words,

> *"An unweeded garden*
> *that grows to seed."*

Shakespeare's plays reflect the shift from optimism to pessimism in Elizabethan society. All his early plays, even the histories and the tragedy *Romeo and Juliet*, have an exuberance that sets them apart from the later works. After 1600, Shakespeare's dramas show the confused, gloomy and often bitter social attitudes of the time. During this period, he wrote his greatest tragedies. Even the comedies *Measure for Measure* and *All's Well That Ends Well* have a bitter quality not found in his earlier comedies. A character in the tragedy *King Lear* cries out in despair,

> *"Alf flies to wanton boys are we to the gods.*
> *They kill us for their sport."*

These lines reflect the uncertainties of the times well as the uncertainties of a particular dramatic situation.

Elizabethan literature mirrored the violence and death so characteristic of English life. Shakespeare's tragedies, like other

Elizabethan tragedies, involve the murder or suicide of many of the leading characters. What is strange is that in spite of their tolerance of cruelty, Elizabethans were extremely sensitive to beauty and grace. They loved many forms of literature, including poetic drama, narrative and lyric poetry, prose fiction and essays. People of all classes enjoyed music and English composers rivalled the finest composers in all Europe. Instrumental music, singing and dancing are important ingredients of Elizabethan drama. Some of Shakespeare's romantic comedies might almost be called "musical comedies". *Twelfth Night,* for example, includes instrumental serenades and rousing drinking songs as well as other songs ranging from sad to comic. Dances form part of the action in *The Tempest, The Winter's Tale* and *Romeo and Juliet.*

Critics' Ranking of Shakespeare's Plays

The nine plays most often read in English language high schools are *Macbeth, As You Like It, Julius Caesar, Hamlet, The Merchant of Venice, A Midsummer Night's Dream, Romeo and Juliet, The Tempest* and *Twelfth Night.* It forms a good list for new readers of Shakespeare too.

Another useful guide for reading and studying the plays is the list given here. It shows how the critics have ranked them throughout the past 350 years. The plays are numbered in the order of their excellence within each group. It is a general summary of critics only. Individual critics have departed widely from some of these estimates.

Among the tragedies, we find:

1. *Hamlet, Macbeth, King Lear, Othello.*
2. *Antony and Cleopatra, Coriolanus, Romeo and Juliet, Julius Caesar.*
3. *Richard II, Richard III, Timon of Athens.*
4. *King John, Titus Andronicus, Henry VI.*

The comedies are:

1. *The Tempest, As You Like It, The Winter's Tale, The Merchant of Venice, Twelfth Night, Much Ado about Nothing, Cymbeline, A Midsummer Night's Dream.*
2. *The Merry Wives of Windsor, The Taming of the Shrew, Two Gentlemen of Verona, All's Well that Ends Well, A Comedy of Errors, Pericles, Love's Labour's Lost, Two Noble Kinsmen.*

The histories are:

Henry IV, Parts 1 and 2, *Henry V, Richard II, Richard III, Henry VIII, King John, Henry VI*, Parts 2 and 3, *Henry VI*, Part I.

Bitter comedies are:

Measure for Measure, Troilus and Cressida.

Chapter 13

Shakespeare and Dance

Dance played an important part in Elizabethan and Jacobean life, so it is understandable that Shakespeare would be sensitive to dance. Music, poetry and dance were essentials of Elizabethan education in addition to sterner pursuits. The average Elizabethan was like Overbury's *Fine Gentleman*: "He carried his pumps in his pocket and lest he should make the fiddlers unaware, whistle his own galliard."

Queen Elizabeth I favoured dancing on Sundays. On a visit to Kenilworth in 1557, lords and ladies danced for her on the Sabbath "with lively agility and commendable grace." James I, who followed Elizabeth on the throne, preserved the court dancing although he frowned on the use of tobacco.

Shakespeare used dance in his plays. In *Romeo and Juliet*, the masked dance is an integral part of the action, the catalyst that finally brings Romeo and Juliet together. In *A Midsummer Night's Dream*, the lovers fill the three hours following the history of Pyramus and Thisbe in a bergomask. Part of the plot, but less integral, are the dances in *Henry V* and the Muscovite mask in

Love's Labour's Lost. In *As You Like It* and elsewhere, a dance brings the play to a happy conclusion, following the Elizabethan tradition of bringing a comedy to a close as there was no curtain.

Dance is used to enrich the imagery of Shakespeare's poetry as seen in *A Midsummer Night's Dream* for example:

> *"By paved fountain or by rushy brook,*
> *or on the beached margent of the sea*
> *to dance our ringlets to the whistling wind.*
>
> *Huge leviathans*
> *forsake unsounded depths to dance on sands.*
>
> *If you find him sad*
> *say I am dancing; if in mirth*
> *report that I am sudden sick."*

Shakespeare contains many references to dance of both the courtly and popular kind. The popular English Morris dance is mentioned in *Henry V*: "Whitsun Morris dance" and *All's Well That Ends Well*: "a Morris for May-day"; in *Love's Labour's Lost*: "He will make one in a dance or play the tabor to the Worthies and let them dance the hay"; from *Henry V* on the eve of Agincourt:

> *"They bid us to the English dancing schools,*
> *and teach lovotas high and swift corantos;*
> *saying our grace is only in our heels."*

Chapter 14

Shakespeare's Greatness as a Poet

No other writer in the world is so quotable or so often quoted. He expressed deep thoughts and feelings in words of great beauty or power. In the technical skills of the poet—rhythm, sound, image and metaphor—he remains the greatest of craftsmen. His range is immense. It extends from funny puns to lofty eloquence, from the speech of common men to the language of philosophers.

The meter of Shakespeare's plays is the unrhymed iambic pentameter called blank verse. This was first used in Italy. It was taken up by English poets in the reign of Henry VIII. The University Wits, especially Christopher Marlowe developed it as a dramatic verse form. Shakespeare perfected it. With John Milton, he made it the greatest meter in English. Blank verse is an excellent form for poetic drama. It is just far enough removed from prose. Blank verse is not monotonous and forced as rhymed verse sometimes is. It is more ordered, swift and noble than prose. At the same time it is so flexible that it seems almost as natural as prose if it is well written.

To gain an impression of Shakespeare's power and variety, one needs to read passages as Prospero's speech in *The Tempest*, Act IV, Scene I:

> *"Our revels now are ended. These our actors,*
> *as I foretold you, were all spirits and*
> *are melted into air, into thin air;*
> *and, like the baseless fabric of this vision,*
> *the cloud-capp'd towers, the gorgeous palaces,*
> *the solemn temples, the great globe itself,*
> *yea, all which it inherit, shall dissolve*
> *and, like this insubstantial pageant faded,*
> *leave not a rack behind. We are such stuff*
> *as dreams are made on, and our little life*
> *is rounded with a sleep."*

And then read Lorenzo's speech in the last act of *The Merchant of Venice*:

> *"How sweet the moonlight sleeps upon this bank!*
> *Here will we sit and let the sounds of music*
> *creep in our ears. Soft stillness and the night*
> *become the touches of sweet harmony.*
> *Sit, Jessica. Look how the floor of heaven*
> *is thick inlaid with patines of bright gold.*
> *There's not the smallest orb which thou behold'st*
> *but in his motion like an angel sings*
> *still quiring to the young-ey'd cherubims;*

> *such harmony is in immortal souls;*
> *but whilst this muddy vesture of decay*
> *doth grossly close it in, we cannot hear it."*

Then compare other great passages, such as Shylock's (in *The Merchant of Venice*): "Signior Antonio, many a time and oft"; Mercutio's (in *Romeo and Juliet*):"O, then, I see Queen Mab hath been with you"; *Richard II's*: "No matter where; of comfort no man speak"; *Hamlet's* "How all occasions do inform against me"; Claudio's (in *Measure for Measure*): "Ay, but to die, and go we know not where"; *Othello's*: "Soft you, a word or two before you go"; Jaques's (in *As You Like It*): "A fool, a fool! I met a fool i' the forest"; and Cleopatra's (*in Antony and Cleopatra*): "Give me my robe, put on my crown." Each speech could come naturally from the speaker and from no one else. Each one is very moving. Each has great rhythmic flow and force; yet each is in the same basic pattern.

Shakespeare's love of words sometimes leads him to rant and bombast, pun and quibble. In haste he sometimes writes nonsense. At times his minor characters talk with affectation or without taste. He can be coarse and he sometimes shocks the reader by his lack of feelings. Yet most of his faults were natural to a writer of his time. This age was not ashamed of man's animal nature and it did not doubt man's divinity.

Reasons for Shakespeare's Popularity

Shakespeare had a magic of speech and fancy which can be felt but not described. His tolerance and sympathy were great and his mind was healthy. No one else possessed his wide variety, his warmth, his clear-cut vision of evil and his high regard for heroism.

He believed that man could overcome the evil in himself. He said, "We are mixtures of good and evil." His people had astonishing reality. Like real people, they could be great and yet foolish, bad and yet likeable, good and yet faulty. He believed that the world was made up of all kinds of people. He found fools, criminals and madmen fascinating. Shakespeare's people were painted larger than life. They had superhuman energy and grandeur. They stood for mankind in its greatest passions and powers, for good or for evil.

Chapter 15

Shakespeare's Four Periods

Shakespeare's first period of writing was of his apprenticeship. Between the ages of twenty-six and thirty, he was learning his craft. He imitated Roman comedy and tragedy, following the styles of playwrights who came just before him. He may have collaborated with Christopher Marlowe and others. The Senecan tragedy, or "tragedy of blood" was in style at that time, hence Shakespeare too wrote plays in this style.

The plots of these plays tended to follow their sources more mechanically than do the plots of Shakespeare's later works which contain a series of closely related episodes, rather than a closely integrated dramatic structure. In addition, the plays generally emphasised events more than the portrayal of character, employing blank verse and little variations in rhythm. Later he wrote chronicle or historical plays which became popular.

The First Period

In this period, Shakespeare's use of language indicates that he had still been struggling to develop his own flexible poetic style.

For example, his descriptive poetry in this period is apt to be flowery, rather than directly related to the development of the characters or the story.

The Comedy of Errors, a comedy partly based on *Amphitruo* and *Menaechmi*, two comedies by the ancient Roman playwright Plautus, were first performed during the period from 1590 to 1594.

The action first takes place in the ancient Greek city of Ephesus with identical twin brothers being named Antipholus. Each brother has a servant named Dromio, who also happen to be twin brothers. Twins of each set had got separated with one twin and his servant living in Ephesus and the other in Syracuse. After Antipholus and Dromio of Syracuse arrive in Ephesus, a series of mistaken identities and comical mix-ups develop before the twin brothers are reunited.

The Comedy of Errors

This play has little character portrayal or fine poetry but the plot is filled with intrigue and humour, making the play highly effective theatre.

Henry VI, **Parts I, II,** and **III,** partly based on *The Union of the Two Noble and Illustrious Families of Lancaster and York* by the English historian Edward Hall and on the *Chronicles* by the English historian Raphael Holinshed, were first performed during the period 1590 to 1592.

The three parts present a panoramic view of English history in the 1400s. The action begins with the death of King Henry V in 1422 and ends with the Battle of Tewkesbury in 1471. The plays vividly mirror the Wars of the Roses, a series of bloody conflicts between the houses of York and Lancaster for control of the English throne. All the three plays dramatise the plots and counter plots that marked the struggle between the two royal houses.

The plays are confusing to read because of their large and shifting casts of characters but have a greater impact when performed than when read. The constant action, exaggerated language and flashes of brilliant characterisation result in lively historical drama.

Richard III, a history partly based on the *Union of the Two Noble and Illustrious Families of Lancaster and York* by the English historian Edward Hall and on the *Chronicles* by the English historian, Raphael Holinshed, deals with the end of the Wars of the Roses.

The hunchbacked Richard, Duke of Gloucester, confides his villainous plans to the audience in a famous soliloquy that begins,

> *"Now is the winter of our discontent*
> *made glorious summer by this sun of York."*

Richard refers to the success of his brother Edward, Duke of York. Edward has overthrown Henry VI and taken the English throne, but now weak and ill, he rules England as Edward IV. Richard wants to gain the crown for himself. He has his other brother, the Duke of Clarence, murdered. After King Edward dies, Richard seizes the throne as Richard III but soon his allies turn against him and join forces with the Earl of Richmond who defeats Richard's army at the Battle of Bosworth Field, where Richard utters the famous cry, "A horse! A horse! My kingdom for a horse!" as his mount is slain during the battle. Richmond finally kills Richard and takes the throne as King Henry VII.

The character of Richard is a superb theatrical portrayal of total evil, with his wickedness blended with such wit that his plotting becomes a delight to watch. People can be freed from the evil around them only when they themselves live up to the demands they make of their leaders.

The Taming of the Shrew, a comedy based on English playwright George Gascoigne's play of the same name, was probably first performed in 1593.

This play dramatises how Petruchio, a young Italian woos the beautiful but shrewish Katherine, whose biting tongue discourages other suitors. Petruchio marries her and before and after the wedding, he systematically humiliates Katherine to cure her of her temper. After many comical clashes between

The Taming of the Shrew

the two, Petruchio's strategy succeeds and Katherine becomes an obedient wife.

A broad and vigorous comedy, the play provides two outstanding roles in the characters of the battling lovers.

Titus Andronicus, a tragedy possibly based in part on *The History of Titus Andronicus* by an unknown English author was probably first performed about 1594.

The play is a type of melodrama that was popular in Elizabethan theatre. The action set in ancient Rome, involves a series of brutal acts of revenge by the Roman general, Titus Andronicus against the men who had raped his daughter, Lavinia. Shakespeare occasionally lightens the play's bloody sensationalism with effective poetry and characterisation. The evil plots of Aaron the Moor provide most of the interest in an otherwise continuous parade of horror and violence.

The Two Gentlemen of Verona, a comedy partly based on Diana, a story by the Spanish author Jorge de Montemayor and on the *The Book of the Governor* by Sir Thomas Elyot, was probably first performed in 1594.

The play is a comedy of love and friendship set in Italy. Two friends, Valentine and Proteus meet in Milan, but soon become rivals for the love of Silvia, the daughter of the Duke of Milan. Valentine discovers Proteus as his friend is about to force his attentions on Silvia. Proteus repents his action and Valentine forgives him. Valentine then tells his friend that he can have Silvia, but Valentine's

The Two Gentlemen of Veronica

generosity becomes unnecessary. Proteus learns that Julia, his former mistress has followed him to Milan disguised as a page. Proteus realises that he really loves Julia and marries her while Valentine marries Silvia.

Shakespeare introduced several features and devices that he later used effectively in the great romantic comedies of his second period. For example, he included beautiful songs, such as "Who is Silvia?"; scenes in a peaceful, idyllic forest; and a girl, disguised as a page, braving the dangers of the world.

King John, a history probably based in part on the *The Troublesome Reign of John* by an unknown English author was probably first performed about 1594.

The story concerns the efforts of England's King John to defend his throne against the claims of Arthur, the young Duke of Brittany. The powerful king of France supports Arthur. John has the allegiance of the brave and able Philip Faulconbridge and of the English nobility. Over time, John's evil and weak policies cost him the loyalty of his followers and both Arthur and John die violently. John's son then takes the throne as Henry III.

The most interesting character is Faulconbridge, whose sarcastic and witty comments on the personalities and motives of the other characters provide the play's best dialogue.

The Second Period

During his second period, Shakespeare brought historical drama and Elizabethan romantic comedy to near perfection, demonstrating his genius for weaving various dramatic actions into a unified plot, rather than writing a series of loosely connected episodes. Throughout the second period, Shakespeare moved steadily towards the matchless gift of characterisation that marks the great tragedies he produced in the early 1600s.

A Midsummer Night's Dream, a comedy probably based on several sources, was probably first performed in 1595.

The play begins with the wedding of Theseus, Duke of Athens with Hippolyta, but most of the action takes place in an enchanted forest where two young men, Lysander and Demetrius, and two young women, Hermia and Helena, wander together after getting lost. Lysander and Demetrius both love Hermia and ignore Helena, who loves Demetrius. Oberon, king of the fairies, orders the mischievous elf, Punch, to anoint Demetrius's eyes with magic drops that will make him love Helena. However, Puck mistakenly anoints Lysander's eyes, creating much comic confusion. Puck finally straightens out the mix-up.

In this play Shakespeare wrote some of his most richly descriptive poetry. Oberon tells Puck,

"I know a bank where the wild thyme blows

where oxlips and the nodding violet grow."

The passage transports the audience to a magical wood where flowers bloom and fairies play. Gaily but firmly, the play makes fun of romantic love as Puck comments,

"Lord, what fools these mortal be!"

Richard II, a history partly based on the *Chronicles* by the English historian Raphael Holinshed was probably first performed in 1595.

As the play begins, King Richard exiles his cousin Bolingbroke from England and confiscates his property. Bolingbroke returns to England and demands his property. Richard has to contend with his cousin's army of nobles while indulging in self-pity. He gives up his crown to Bolingbroke without a fight. Richard is put in prison while Bolingbroke is crowned Henry IV. The imprisoned Richard is killed by a knight and at the end of the play, Henry vows to make a journey to the Holy Land to pay for Richard's death.

In this play Shakespeare seriously explored the idea that a person's character determines his fate. The play is a study of a weak, self-centred man, Richard, who becomes so out of touch with reality that his only defence of his kingdom is the hope that his "master, God omnipotent,

Is mustering in his clouds on our behalf

Armies of pestilence."

When he faces the certain loss of his crown, Richard can only compare himself to Christ, who "in twelve,

Found truth in all but one; I, in twelve thousand none."

Love's Labour's Lost, a comedy based on many sources was probably first performed in 1596. King Ferdinand of Navarre and his friends Berowne, Longaville and Dumain vow to live without the company of women for three years. But the princess of France unexpectedly arrives at the king's court

Love's Labour's Lost

with three female companions. The comedy centres on the efforts of the men to woo the women while pretending to keep their vow. At the play's end, women propose to their visitors, who promise to give their answer in a year and a day.

This witty comedy has more references to events of the day than do any of Shakespeare's other plays. Many of these references have lost their meaning for modern audiences as its numerous passages are difficult to understand. In addition, much of the language is elaborate and artificial. But Shakespeare included two simple and lovely songs—"When daisies pied and violent blue" and "When icicles hang by the wall". This play also has handsome scenes of spectacle and several entertaining comic characters.

Romeo and Juliet, is a tragedy whose essential theme is taken from the common currency of European literature. The story of the "pair of star-crossed lovers" driven to destruction by the strife between their parents' families had been told many times in many forms during the two centuries before Shakespeare brought it to

Romeo and Juliet

Juliet

the stage. Based on *Romeus and Juliet*, a poem by the English author Arthur Brooke, it was first performed in 1596 probably. Within a few years, Shakespeare's version quickly became "the" version of *Romeo and Juliet*.

Two teenaged lovers are caught in a bitter feud between their families, the Montagues and the Capulets. Romeo, a Monatague and his friends crash into a masked ball given by the Capulets. After the ball, Romeo meets Juliet, a Capulet and they fall in love. The next day, the couple is secretly married by Friar Laurence. Returning from the wedding, Romeo meets Juliet's cousin Tybalt, who tries to pick a fight with him. But Romeo refuses to fight his new relative. To defend the Montague honour, Romeo's friend Mercutio accepts Tybalt's challenge. As Romeo attempts to part the young men, Tybalt stabs Mercutio to death. In revenge, Romeo then fights and kills Tybalt. As a result of the death of Tybalt, Romeo is sent into exile.

Juliet's father forces Juliet to marry her cousin Paris, unaware that she is already married. Here Friar Laurence gives Julie a drug that puts her into a death-like sleep for forty-two hours. The friar sends a messenger to the exiled Romeo to tell him of the drug, but the messenger is delayed. Romeo hears that Julie is dead and rushes to the tomb where she is placed. Here, he takes poison and dies by Juliet's side. Juliet awakens to find her husband dead and stabs herself. The discovery of the dead lovers convinces the two families that they must end their feud.

During this period Shakespeare shows ease, power and maturity and the plays are generally sunny and full of joyous poetry. Shakespeare shows sympathy for the young people and blames the tragic ending on the blind self-interest of the adults. The effective characterisation and intensely lyrical poetry, though frequently artificial, shows Shakespeare's use of simpler language and a more direct style that is used in his later tragedies. For example, as Romeo watches Juliet on the balcony outside her bedroom, he sighs:

> *"See how she leans her cheek up on her hand!*
> *Oh, that I were a glove upon that hand,*
> *that I might touch that cheek!"*

The Merchant of Venice, a comedy partly based on *Il Pecorone*, a collection of tales by Giovanni Fiorentino, was probably first performed in 1597.

Antonio, a merchant in Venice borrows money from the Jewish moneylender Shylock to whom he promises a pound of his flesh in case he fails to repay the loan in three months. Antonio cannot pay back and Shylock demands his pound of flesh. An heiress Portia disguises herself as a learned lawyer and pleads on Antonio's behalf. Portia then warns Shylock that he may take Antonio's flesh but not his blood and if he were to spill any blood when taking flesh, he would have to forsake all his property. Shylock drops his demand and Antonio is saved.

Here comic intrigue is combined with hatred and greed. Though the ending his happy, it is not a light-hearted comedy. In Shakespeare's era, both the church and the State

The Merchant of Venice

considered money lending on high interest a crime. Shylock was thus a natural object of scorn but Shakespeare shows him sympathetically particularly when Shylock asks, "If you prick us, do we not bleed? If you tickle us, do we not laugh? If you poison us, do we not die? And if you wrong us, shall we not revenge?"

Henry IV, Parts I and II, partly based on the *Chronicles* by the English historian Raphael Holinshed were probably first staged in 1597 to 1598.

In Part I, the guilt-ridden Henry IV wants to go to the Holy Land in repentance for Richard's death, but political unrest prevents him. At the same time, Prince Hal, his son, leads an apparently irresponsible life with his brawling friends, but at the Battle of Shrewsbury, Hal reveals himself to be a brave and princely warrior. Part II is more memorable as it introduces Falstaff as bragging, lying and thievish drunkard whose faults are balanced by his sharp humour, his contagious love of life and refusal to take either himself or the world seriously. His ironical comment is, "I am not only witty in myself, but the cause that wit is in other men."

As You Like It, a comedy partly based on *Rosalynde* by Thomas Lodge was probably first performed on stage in 1599.

Rosalind and her cousin Celia leave the court of Celia's father, who is a Duke, after he unjustly banishes Rosalind. Accompanied by Touchstone, the court jester, the two girls take

As You Like It

refuge in the Forest of Arden. Rosalind disguised as a young shepherd named Ganymede meets Orlando and not recognising the disguised girl, Orlando pretends that Ganymede is Rosalind, so he can practice his declarations of love. Rosalind finally reveals her identity and marries Orlando. The news that Rosalind's father has been restored to his dukedom completes the comedy's happy ending.

Like most Elizabethan romantic comedies, this play concerns young lovers who pursue their happy destiny in a world seemingly far removed from reality. Although evil threatens, it never does harm. Shakespeare has enriched the play with beautiful poetry as well as several charming songs.

Henry V, a history partly based on the *Chronicles* by the English historian Raphael Holinshed and partly on the *The Famous Victories of Henry the Fifth* by an unknown author, was probably first performed in 1599.

This play continues with the action of *Henry IV*, Part II and presents an idealised portrait of England's King Henry V, who leads his army to victory and lays claim to the French throne. There he is promised the throne and the hand of Katherine, the French princess with whom he has fallen in love.

The play consists of loosely related episodes unified by the character of the brave but modest king. The king's patriotic speech is very encouraging: "Once more unto the breach, dear friends, once more." This speech concludes with the king saying,

"The game's afoot!

Follow your spirit; and upon this charge cry, 'God for Harry, England and Saint George!'"

Julius Caesar, a tragedy partly based on *Lives* by the ancient Greek biographer Plutarch, was supposedly first performed in 1599.

The play takes place in ancient Rome and has Brutus, a Roman general and Caesar's best friend as the central character. Brutus, in a plot to murder Caesar, attacks Caesar who resists until he sees Brutus. Caesar's last words are, "Et tu, Brute? [You too, Brutus?] Then fall, Caesar!" Brutus then defends the assassination to a crowd of Romans but allows the clever and eloquent Mark Antony to deliver a funeral speech over Caesar's body. Antony tells the people, "I come to bury Caesar, not to praise him," and describes the plotters as "honourable men". As the crowd gets incited to avenge Caesar's death, the plotters flee Rome. Mark Antony leads an army that defeats the forces of the plotters and Brutus commits suicide. Antony says over his corpse,

Julius Caesar

"This was the noblest Roman of them all as the other plotters killed Caesar out of envy but only Brutus acted with honest thought

And common good to all."

This became a popular play because of its magnificent language and sharp character delineation. A thoughtful withdrawn man, Brutus is torn between his affection for Caesar and his strong sense of duty to the State.

Much Ado About Nothing, a comedy partly based on *Orlando Furioso* and partly on a story in *Novelle*, both by Italian authors, was probably performed in 1599.

The villainous Don John slanders the virtue of Hero, the daughter of the governor of Messina. After a great deal of intrigue, the play ends happily. However, the real interest centres on the relationship between Beatrice and Benedick, two witty young people who trade insults throughout the play. Their arguments and their final discovery that they love each other provide much of the fun.

Much Ado About Nothing

Twelfth Night, a comedy partly based on *Farewell to Military Profession* by English author Barnabe Riche, was first performed in 1600.

Viola and Sebastian, who are twins, get separated during a shipwreck. Viola gets stranded and disguises herself as Cesario, a page and enters the service of Duke Orsino, who sends her to woo Countess Olivia for him. But the countess falls in love with Cesario who, in turn, falls in love with the Duke. The romantic action alternates with scenes of realistic comedy. The plot

Twelfth Night

thickens when Sebastian, Viola's twin brother appears. Viola then reveals her identity and the confusion is resolved. The comedy also contains the famous passage: "Some are born great, some achieve greatness and some have greatness thrust upon 'em."

Here Shakespeare creates a perfect blend of sentiment and humour. In addition he makes the clown makes witty comments on the foolish ways of the people.

The Merry Wives of Windsor, a comedy based on an unknown source or sources was first performed in 1600.

It is said that since Queen Elizabeth enjoyed the comic character John Falstaff in *Henry IV* plays, she asked Shakespeare to write a comedy portraying Falstaff in love. Falstaff's efforts to make love to two middle-class housewives in the town of Windsor end in him becoming a victim of a number of comical tricks invented by the women.

Though lacking in romantic poetry as seen in most of Shakespearean comedies, the play is highly entertaining. Falstaff remains theatrically effective, even though the audience laughs at him rather than with him as in the earlier plays.

The Third Period

With *Hamlet*, written in about 1601, Shakespeare's third period begins. For eight years he probed the problem of evil in the world. At times he reached an almost desperate pessimism. Even the two comedies of this period—*All's Well That Ends Well* and *Measure for Measure*—are more disturbing than amusing. The plays in this period, except possibly for *Pericles*, are in many ways the darkest of Shakespeare's career and address issues such as betrayal, murder, lust, power and egoism. During this period, Shakespeare's language shows remarkable variety and flexibility, moving back and forth between verse and prose. His language is a dramatic tool that makes possible the skilful psychological portraits which mark this period.

Hamlet, a tragedy partly based on *Hamlet*, a lost play by an unknown English author and on *Histoires Tragiques* by French author, Francois de Belleforest, was probably first staged in 1601.

Prince Hamlet deeply mourns the recent death of his father as also the subsequent remarriage of his mother to his Uncle Claudius. The ghost of Hamlet's father appears to the prince and tells him he was murdered by Claudius. The ghost demands that Hamlet take revenge on the king. Hamlet decides to have a band of travelling actors perform "something like the murder of my father" before the king to see if Claudius will show any guilt. The king's violent reaction to the play betrays his guilt. Polonius, the king's advisor is killed by Hamlet for which the latter is sent into exile. Hamlet, however, returns to Denmark and sees the burial of the girl he had loved. The girl's brother challenges Hamlet to a duel where the latter gets wounded by a poisoned weapon. Hamlet's mother accidentally drinks from a cup of poisoned

Hamlet

wine and Hamlet kills Claudius. At the end of the play, Hamlet, his mother and Claudius die.

Shakespeare handled the complex plot brilliantly and perhaps created his greatest gallery of characters. The role of Hamlet is considered one of the theatre's greatest acting challenges. The deep conflict within the thoughtful and idealistic Hamlet, as he is torn between the demands of his emotions and the hesitant scepticism of his mind, is expressed in his words: "To be, or not to be".

Troilus and Cressida, a tragedy based on several sources was first performed in 1602.

The play dramatises the love of the Trojan warrior Troilus for the unfaithful Cressida. The couple pledges their love, but Cressida is unexpectedly sent to the Greek camp in exchange for a Trojan prisoner where she falls in love with a Greek warrior. The play ends with the death of Troilus's brother.

In spite of its heroic setting, the play is neither noble nor stirring.

All's Well That Ends Well, a comedy partly based on *The Palace of Pleasure* by William Painter was probably first performed in 1603.

Helena falls in love with Bertram, a nobleman. Helena cures the French king of an illness and wins Bertram as her husband in reward. But Bertram considers her beneath him socially and deserts her. He tells her

All's Well That Ends Well

in a letter that only if she was to get a ring from his finger and become pregnant by him, would he accept her as his wife. One night she takes the place of a girl on whom Bertram had a foolish crush. It is only later that Bertram realises his mistake and promises to be faithful to his wife Helena.

Unlike Shakespeare's earlier comedies, this play has little gaiety and romance. Is interest lies primarily in the playwright's efforts to express through comedy his troubled view of humanity's imperfections.

Measure for Measure, a comedy partly based on *Promos and Cassandra* by George Whetstone, was first performed in 1604.

The Duke of Vienna turns over the affairs of the city to his stern deputy and a wise old nobleman in the hope of introducing the much needed moral reforms. In one of his first acts, the deputy Angelo sentences Claudio to death for making his fiancée pregnant. Claudio's sister pleads for her brother's life. Stricken by her beauty, Angelo

Measure for Measure

promises provided she allows him to make love to her. She refuses to yield her honour. After much intrigue and plotting, Claudio is saved and the sister keeps her virtue intact.

Many critics consider the ending weak with the first part deadly serious and the latter becoming a typical romantic intrigue.

However, in spite of its flaws, its dramatic poetry at times equals that of the best seen in Shakespeare's tragedies.

Othello, a tragedy partly based on *Hecatommithi* by Cinthio, an Italian, was first performed in 1604.

Othello, a soldier becomes a general and marries Desdemona, a beautiful Venetian girl but is sent to Cyprus where his villainous aide decides to destroy the general. He fills his mind with false stories about Desdemona till the general in anger murders Desdemona. When he learns that he has been tricked by his aide, Othello kills himself, describing himself as "one that loved not wisely, but too well."

Othello

This play is a downright tragedy with the action moving rapidly and the language simple and direct, like the main character. It is a tragedy of personal tensions, of love and hatred and of jealousy and impatience.

King Lear, a tragedy based on the *Chronicles* by Raphael Holinshed, *The True Chronicle History of King Lear* by an unknown author and *Arcadia* by Sir Philip Sidney, was first performed in 1605.

The plot concerns King Lear who prepares to divide his kingdom among his three daughters—Regan, Goneril and Cordelia. One day Cordelia displeases her father who disinherits her. Soon Regan and Goneril show their ingratitude and force Lear to spend a night outdoors during a storm. He becomes insane and Cordelia returns to find her father insane and helps him recover. Armies raised by the wicked two elder sisters capture Lear and Cordelia and the latter is put to death. King Lear dies of a broken heart as he kneels over the dead body of his daughter.

The brilliant characterisations with the characters realising their mistake reflect Shakespeare's basic optimism. But they do so too late to prevent their destruction and that of the people around them. This in reality was Shakespeare's tragic view of humanity.

Macbeth, a tragedy partly based on the *Chronicles* by Raphael Holinshed was first performed in 1606.

On returning from a battle, Macbeth meets some witches who predict that he would first become a baron and then king of Scotland. He becomes a baron alright and in his hurry to become king, he murders King Duncan, a guest in his castle. Macbeth seizes the

Macbeth

throne of Scotland. But Macbeth finds no peace as the witches predict that Banquo's descendants would be kings of Scotland. Macbeth gets Banquo killed but his son escapes. Having become a hardened killer, he orders the killing of his enemy Macduff but the latter kills Macbeth in battle. Duncan's son is proclaimed the King of Scotland.

In *Macbeth*, Shakespeare wrote the tragedy of man's conscience and how a person changes from strong but imperfect moral sense to become a man who will stop at nothing to get and keep what he wants. He becomes so hardened that he is unable to react to his wife's death except to say that life is only "a tale told by an idiot, full of sound and fury, signifying nothing."

Macbeth's wife encourages murder in the beginning, but later her conscience pricks as her husband's hardens. The play is noted for its bitter humour, which reinforces the tragic action.

Timon of Athens, a tragedy based on *Lives* by ancient Greek biographer Plutarch, was probably first performed in 1607.

Timon is a nobleman in ancient Athens surrounded by flatterers. He spends his money without discretion, becomes penniless, his friends desert him, is forced to leave Athens and go and live in a cave where he finds a buried treasure. But his new-found wealth brings him no pleasure and he dies a bitter man.

The play has passages of great eloquence and depicts people at their worst, with few honourable qualities that lighten the gloom.

Pericles, partly based on *Confessio Amantis* retold by John Gower, was first performed in 1607.

The plot deals with the marriage of Prince Pericles, the loss of his wife and daughter and their rediscovery. The most moving scene is at the end of the play when Pericles and Marina meet and recognise each other after years of separation.

Considered uneven in quality, scholars doubt how much of it was written by Shakespeare, though the majority believes he wrote it.

Antony and Cleopatra, based on *Lives* by Plutarch was first performed in 1607.

Mark Antony rules over Egypt where he takes the Egyptian queen Cleopatra as his mistress. Political problems and death of his wife force Antony to return to Rome where he marries Octavia for political reasons. Soon he returns to "his Egyptian dish". But Octavia's brother draws him into a battle at sea where Cleopatra's fleet deserts him and Antony flees. A second battle follows and again Cleopatra's ship deserts him and thinking that she is dead, he stabs himself. Cleopatra presses a poisonous snake to her breast and dies of its bite.

The characters of Antony and Cleopatra are at variance. At one

Antony and Cleopatra

Cleopatra

level they live for pleasure alone and at another, they are tragic characters willing to risk kingdoms for their love.

Coriolanus, a tragedy based on *Lives* by Plutarch, was first performed in 1608.

On capturing Corioli, Marcius is named Coriolanus and he returns to Rome. To be made consul, he has to win the support of the common people whom he abhors. His condescending attitude leads him to his exile. He joins forces with his old enemy Aufidius to attack Rome. His mother, wife and son beg him to spare the city and he withdraws but Aufidius denounces him and has him murdered.

This tragedy questions the value of personal popularity and political success. It also debates the conflicting interests of public and private life.

The Fourth Period

In his fourth and last period Shakespeare uses a new form. It was the tragicomedy, or dramatic romance. Turning romance to tragicomedy, he wrote three more major plays: *Cymbeline*, *The Winter's Tale* and *The Tempest*. Less bleak than the tragedies, these plays are graver in tone than the comedies of the 1590s, but they end with reconciliation and forgiveness of potentially tragic errors. Some commentators have seen this change in mood as evidence of a more serene view of life on Shakespeare's part, but may merely reflect the theatrical fashion of the day. Shakespeare collaborated on two further surviving plays, *Henry VIII* and *The Two Noble Kinsmen*, probably with John Fletcher. In his hands the tragicomedy is calm, sober and quietly lovely. *The Tempest* is perhaps the most beautiful and serene of all his plays. These plays bear similarities to medieval romance literature. Among the features of these plays are the redemptive plotline with a happy ending and magic and other fantastic elements.

Cymbeline, a tragedy partly based on *Lives* by Plutarch, was first performed in 1608.

King Cymbeline exiles the poor Posthumous after he marries Imogen, the king's daughter. The treacherous Iachimo tries to make love to Imogen but she turns him down, though he makes Posthumous believe that Imogen allowed him to do so. Imogen tries to get her killed but she escapes and after many adventures, the husband and wife are united.

The characters are vividly sketched, particularly Imogen who is a most appealing heroine of this lively melodramatic plot.

The Winter's Tale, based on *Pandosto* by Robert Greene, was first performed in 1610.

King Leontes becomes jealous of his faithful wife Hermione and has her imprisoned. He gets their newborn daughter abandoned in an isolated place. Finally he realises that he is wrong. Meanwhile his daughter grows up into a beautiful girl and falls in love with Florizel but has to flee to Leontes's court

The Winter's Tale

for protection. Leontes discovers that the girl is his daughter and he accepts her. He gets united with his wife too who had so far been living alone.

Like *Cymbeline*, this play concerns exile, women suffering from male jealousy and the reuniting of loved ones. Beginning with destruction, the tale stresses on rebuilding of relationships.

The Tempest, probably based on several sources, was first performed in 1611.

Prospero, exiled from Italy, lives on an island with his daughter Miranda. Being a magician, Prospero causes a ship carrying his enemies to be wrecked from which Prince Ferdinand escapes. Miranda falls in love with him and cries out, "O, brave new world that hath such creatures in it." Prospero, with his magic, brings the two lovers together and upsets the plot hatched against him by his shipwrecked enemies. Prospero appears before his enemies and forgives them.

In this play the old injuries are forgiven and the characters begin a new and happier life. Shakespeare has blended spectacle, song and dance into a brilliant dramatic fantasy.

Henry VIII, based on the *Chronicles* by Raphael Holinshed and *The Book of Martyrs* by John Foxe, was first performed in 1613.

The play deals with King Henry VIII's annulment of his marriage to Catherine and his marriage to Anne Boleyn.

This is a loosely constructed drama better known for it pageantry than for its characterisation. It has passages of splendid verse but the work does not do credit to Shakespeare.

Poems

Shakespeare wrote two long poems—*Venus and Adonis* and *The Rape of Lucrece* apart from the *Sonnets*.

Venus and Adonis, is partly based on *Metamorphoses* by Ovid and tells how Venus, the Goddess of Love, tries to win the love of a handsome mortal Adonis. He resists her but is finally killed by a wild boar while hunting.

The poem is witty and filled with sexual references and is noted for its vivid settings and elaborate speeches.

The Rape of Lucrece, based on the works of Ovid and other authors, talks of Lucrece, the virtuous wife of a Roman nobleman. She is sexually assaulted by General Tarquin after which, Lucrece demands that her husband and his friends would swear to destroy the culprit. She then kills herself.

This poem is more serious in tone than *Venus and Adonis* and has little action but depends chiefly on long flowery speeches for its effect.

Categorisation of Shakespeare's Works

Comedies

- *All's Well That Ends Well*
- *As You Like It*
- *The Comedy of Errors*
- *Love's Labour's Lost*
- *Measure for Measure*
- *The Merry Wives of Windsor*
- *A Midsummer Night's Dream*
- *Much Ado About Nothing*
- *Pericles, Prince of Tyre*
- *The Taming of the Shrew*
- *The Tempest*
- *Twelfth Night or What you Will*
- *The Two Gentlemen of Verorna*
- *The Two Noble Kinsmen*
- *The Winter's Tale*

Histories

- *King John*
- *Richard II*
- *Henry IV,* Part 1
- *Henry IV,* Part 2
- *Henry V*
- *Henry VI,* Part 1

- *Henry VI*, Part 2
- *Henry VI*, Part 3
- *Richard III*
- *Henry VIII*

Tragedies

- *Romeo and Juliet*
- *Coriolanus*
- *Titus Andronicus*
- *Timon of Athens*
- *Julius Caesar*
- *Macbeth*
- *Hamlet*
- *Troilus and Cressida*
- *King Lear*
- *Othello*
- *Antony and Cleopatra*
- *Cymbeline*

Poems

- *Shakespeare's Sonnets*
- *Venus and Adonis*
- *The Rape of Lucrece*
- *The Passionate Pilgrim*
- *The Phoenix and the Turtle*
- *A Lover's Complaint*

Lost Plays

- *Love's Labour's Won*
- *Cardenio*

Apocrypha

- *Arden of Faversham*
- *The Birth of Merlin*
- *Locrine*
- *The London Prodigal*
- *The Puritan*
- *The Second Maiden's Tragedy*
- *Sir John Oldcastle*
- *Thomas Lord Cromwell*
- *A Yorkshire Tragedy*
- *Edward III*
- *Sir Thomas More*

Chapter 16

Shakespeare's Influence

Shakespeare has had enormous influence on later theatre, literature and culture throughout the world. His works have helped shape the literature of all English-speaking countries as of other countries too. In particular he expanded the dramatic potential of characterisation, plot, language and genre. He also contributed greatly to the development of the English language. He freely experimented with grammar and vocabulary and so helped prevent literary English from becoming fixed and artificial.

Shakespeare's influence on language has been tied to writers and scholars. As far as scholars can tell, Shakespeare also invented such common words as "assassination", "bump", "eventful" and "lonely".

Many people can identify lines and passages as Shakespeare's even though they have never seen or read any of his plays. Examples include: "To be, or not to be", "Friends, Romans, countrymen, lend me your ears" and "A horse! A horse! My kingdom for a horse!"

Shakespeare's works have made a lasting impression on subsequent literature as for example, romance had not been viewed as a worthy topic for tragedy. Soliloquies had been used mainly to convey information about characters or events, but Shakespeare used them to explore his characters' minds. His work heavily influenced later poetry too. The romantic poets attempted to revive Shakespearean verse drama, though with little success. Critic George Steiner described all English verse dramas from Coleridge to Tennyson as "feeble variations on Shakespearean themes."

Shakespeare influenced novelists such as Thomas Hardy, William Faulkner and Charles Dickens; the latter often quoted from Shakespeare's works. Shakespeare's grammar and spellings were less standardised then than they are now and his use of language helped shape modern English. Samuel Johnson quotes him more often than any other author in his *A Dictionary of the English Language*, the first serious work of its type. Expressions such as "with bated breath" in *Merchant of Venice* and "a foregone conclusion" from *Othello* have found their way into everyday English speech.

Playwright Ben Jonson wrote, "He was not of an age, but for all time," to describe his friend William Shakespeare and how right he was. Over the years, styles of acting and staging plays have changed many times but Shakespeare has not gone out of fashion. His plays have been translated into almost every language and are still being performed all around the globe. They have inspired ballets, operas, musicals, films and paintings. Shakespeare's other great legacy is to the English language itself. Hundreds of everyday words and phrases appeared first in Shakespeare's plays, including "bare-faced", cold-blooded", "excitement" and "fair play". We all regularly quote from Shakespeare without realising it.

Chapter 17

Authorship

About 150 years after Shakespeare's death, doubts began to be expressed about the authorship of the plays and poetry attributed to him. Researchers who believe the works to have been written by another playwright, or a group of playwrights, have since then proposed many candidates for alternative authorship, including Francis Bacon, Christopher Marlowe and Edward de Vere, the Earl of Oxford. While it is generally accepted in academic circles that Shakespeare's plays were written by Shakespeare of Stratford, popular interest in the subject, particularly the Oxfordian theory, has continued into the 21st century.

Shakespeare's reputation as a poet is confirmed in 1598 when Francis Meres attacked him as being "mellifluous" and described his work as honey-tongued, "sugared sonnets among his private friends" in his own *Palladis Tamia* of 1598.

The proof most often cited that Shakespeare authored his plays, however, was the *First Folio* (1623) where Henry Condell and John Hemminges, who were actors in the bard's theatre company, claim in a dedicatory verse within the *Folio* that they recorded and collected his plays as a memorial to the late actor and playwright. In terms of value, the *First Folio*, originally was sold for one pound in 1623. Today as one of just 250 still in existence, it would fetch nearly three million US dollars.

Further proof of authorship comes in the form of a poem by Ben Jonson, one of the bard's more friendly rivals, who criticises the playwright's dramatic plays. It is contained within a work entitled *Discoveries* (also known as *Timber*) dated 1641. Despite his criticism Ben Jonson paradoxically also said that Stratford's famous bard's works were timeless, describing them as "not of an age, but for all time."

Long after Shakespeare was dead and subsequent elevated icon status, rumours began to circulate. We can never know which plays were well received and which flopped as records are not available. Ultimately Shakespeare's greatest failure lies in his failure to confirm that he wrote the plays. The man we know as William Shakespeare couldn't have written all those plays, many have argued. He was too uneducated, too unworldly. Or was he not? Only Shakespeare could have answered that one, but the controversy continues to rage nearly 400 years later.

List of Plays with Probable Date of Writing

1590	:	*Henry VI*, Part One
1590	:	*The Comedy of Errors*
1590	:	*Titus Andronicus*
1590-92	:	*Henry VI*, Parts Two and Three
1591	:	*Richard III*
1591-98	:	*King John*
1592	:	*The Taming of the Shrew*
1592-93	:	*The Two Gentlemen of Verona*
1595	:	*Richard II*
1595	:	*A Midsummer Night's Dream*
1595	:	*Romeo and Juliet*
1595	:	*Love's Labour's Lost*
1596-98	:	*The Merchant of Venice*
1597	:	*As You Like It*
1597	:	*Henry IV*, Part One
1597	:	*Henry IV*, Part Two
1597	:	*The Merry Wives of Windsor*
1598-99	:	*Much Ado About Nothing*
1599	:	*Henry V*
1599	:	*Julius Caesar*
1599-1601	:	*Hamlet*

1601	:	*Twelfth Night*
1602	:	*Troilus and Cressida*
1602-04	:	*Othello*
1603-04	:	*All's Well That Ends Well*
1604	:	*Measure for Measure*
1604-65	:	*King Lear*
1606	:	*Macbeth*
1606, 1607	:	*Antony and Cleopatra*
1606-08	:	*Pericles, Prince of Tyre*
1607	:	*Timon of Athens*
1608	:	*Coriolanus*
1609-10	:	*Cymbeline*
1610-11	:	*The Winter's Tale*
1611	:	*The Tempest*

Principal Facts of Shakespeare's Life

1564 : Born at Stratford-upon-Avon, Warwickshire, probably April 21st-23rd and baptised

1582, April 26th : Licence issued for his marriage with Anne Hathaway of Shottery

1583 : Birth of daughter Susanna

1585 : Twins, a boy named Hamnet and a girl named Judith, born

1592 : First alluded to in a book by Robert Greene

1593 : *Venus and Adonis* published

1594 : Shakespeare becomes member of the Lord Chamberlain's Men acting company

1594 : *The Rape of Lucrece* published

1595 : *A Midsummer Night's Dream* first performed possibly on stage

1596 : *Romeo and Juliet* first performed probably

1596 : His son Hamnet dies

1596 : His father is granted a coat of arms

1597 : Purchases New Place in Stratford

1597 : *The Merchant of Venice* first performed possibly

1598 : *Henry IV*, Parts I and II, probably first staged

1598 : Praised by Francis Meres, who mentions his poems and sonnets and twelve of his plays

1599 : Becomes part owner of Globe Theatre in London

1600 : First performance of *Twelfth Night*

1601 : *Hamlet* probably first staged

1603 : Shakespeare becomes member of the King's Men acting company

1603 : Shakespeare and fellow players honoured by King James I

1604 : *Othello* performed for first time

1605 : *King Lear* probably first performed

1606 : *Macbeth* performed first time

1607 : Daughter Susanna marries

1607 : *Antony and Cleopatra* probably first performed

1609 : His sonnets published

1611 : *The Tempest* probably first performed

1613 : Globe Theatre burned down during staging of *Henry VIII*

1616 : Daughter Judith marries

1616 : He dies in Stratford on April 23rd and buried on April 25th

1623 : His collection of plays, *The First Folio* published by his fellow actors

1670 : His last direct descendant, a granddaughter, dies

Chief Facts of the World during Shakespeare's Period

1559 : Elizabeth I occupies the British throne

1563 : Church of England established

1578 : Chinese population reaches sixty million

1580 : Francis Drake circles the globe

1587 : American colony of Virginia named after Elizabeth I

1588 : England defeats the Spanish Armada

1593 : Plague in England

1601 : Essex rebellion

1603 : Queen Elizabeth dies

1603 : James VI of Scotland becomes James I of England

1603 : First Kabuki theatre in Japan set up

1605 : Gunpowder plot in England

1608 : Plague in England

1609 : Nursery rhyme *Three Blind Mice* published

1612 : Virginia colonists export tobacco

1615 : Hot chocolate introduced in Europe

1619 : First black slaves arrive in Virginia colony

Questions

1. What are the reasons for our knowing so very little about William Shakespeare?

2. What was the other name by which Queen Elizabeth I became famous?

3. What is meant by words like "alderman" and "whittawering"?

4. Why did William Shakespeare give so much importance to securing the coat of arms?

5. Why was school education imparted in Latin to students during the Elizabethan era?

6. Were there any divisions in Christianity in the 16th century?

7. What is a hornbook?

8. How do you think Shakespeare could give such accurate descriptions of flowers, trees, birds and animals in his books?

9. How did Shakespeare develop a fondness for plays during his boyhood?

10. What is the difference between a "shotgun wedding" and "handfast" marriage?

11. What is meant by Shakespeare's "lost years"?

12. How did Londoners pass their time?

13. What does the term "coneycatchers" mean?

14. What is meant by "blank verse"?

15. Write two to three lines on theatre companies.

16. Who were the Lord Chamberlain's Men?

17. Who were anti-Stratfordians?

18. What was the Globe?

19. After the death of Queen Elizabeth I in 1603, who became the ruler of England?

20. Who were the King's Men?

21. What is New Place?

22. What is the mystery surrounding Shakespeare's *Sonnets*?

23. How many plays did Shakespeare write?

24. What makes Shakespeare's use of language so unique and enduring?

25. "He was not of an age, but for all time." Who wrote this about whom?

26. Name four famous tragedies of Shakespeare.

27. What is *First Folio*?

28. What is the meaning of soliloquy?

29. When did Shakespeare die and where?

30. Shakespeare is more famous as a poet, writer, actor or playwright? Please comment.

Answers

1. One of the reasons could be that Shakespeare's countrymen of the time did not bother to keep biographical information which did not pertain either to the church or the State. The other reason might be that it was not realised at that time that Shakespeare would acquire eminence as one of the most leading playwrights of England.

2. As Queen Elizabeth had no interest in war and allowed trade to flourish, England grew more and more prosperous during her reign and because of which she came to be popularly known as "Good Queen Bess".

3. An "alderman" is a senior official in a local council. William Shakespeare's father John Shakespeare became an alderman in 1565.
   "Whittawering" is a process in which white or soft leather is tanned to make items like purses and gloves.

4. The coat of arms is a shield-shaped design with the motto *non sanz droit* engraved on it in Latin. It was wanted by all Englishmen as it increased their social standing and helped them move up the social ladder by being thought of as gentlemen.

5. Knowledge of Latin was necessary for a career in medicine, law or the church. Laws were written in Latin; church services were conducted in Latin. At that time, students were not allowed to speak in English at school. Latin grammar was taught in grammar schools.

6. There were two rival versions of Christianity—Catholicism and Protestantism. The former traditionally descended from the original church before the division with Protestantism occurred. Protestantism too is a branch of Christianity set up in "protest" against Catholicism during the15th century and following the principles of Reformation leaders, such as Luther and Calvin. The Protestants too were further divided into

Anglicans and Puritans with the latter being very strict in lifestyle and considering every form of pleasure as bad.

7. In the 1590s, children learned to read using a hornbook which was a piece of wood covered with printed paper, protected by a sheet of transparent horn. The hornbook, religiously carried in the satchel by the child, was meant for learning the Lord's Prayer in Latin.

8. William Shakespeare's writings were understandably based upon his childhood experiences and love of the countryside In *Macbeth*, when describing the night he writes, "Light thickens and the crow makes wing to the rooky wood."

9. It seems that as a market centre, Stratford was a lively town. Holidays provided pageants and shows including plays. By 1569, travelling companies of professional actors were free going in Stratford which held two fairs every year, attracting visitors from other countries too. Moreover the nearby town of Coventry was famous for staging mystery plays where stages were set up on wagons. Different scenes were performed on each wagon as they rolled through. Possibly young William travelled to see them and got inspired to write and act in plays.

10. "Shotgun wedding" is a marriage forced or required because of pregnancy of the bride-to-be. A "handfast" marriage is one in which a contract or covenant especially of betrothal or marriage is signed.

11. The period from the time Shakespeare left school at about the age of fifteen till 1592, when he was described as an upcoming playwright in London, is known as his "lost years". Many theories are advanced as to what may have happened during the lost years, but most are based on imagination than on facts.

12. Londoners enjoyed watching cruel blood-sports such as fights between bulls, bears and packs of dogs. People often stood and watched executions of traitors. Many people passed their time by gambling at dice and cards, or playing sports such as bowls.

13. "Coneycatchers" were criminals who made a living by cheating at cards and dice. They were on the look out for newcomers from the countryside

like William Shakespeare and called their victims "coneys", meaning rabbits.

14. "Blank verse" is a verse which does not rhyme but has rhythm. Educated men in the 1590s wrote plays in unrhymed lines of ten syllables. For example, Christopher Marlowe wrote: "Is this the face that launched a thousand ships?"

15. Theatre companies were commercial organisations which staged plays, depending on admission tickets for their income. These companies had on their payroll permanent actors who provided a variety of plays, week after week to entertain the public.

16. Lord Chamberlain's Men was a theatre company which had Lord Chamberlain as its patron and thus came to be named after him. The company which performed at the Theatre in north London, was at first owned by James Burbage. This was taken over by Lord Chamberlain and William Shakespeare became one of the several "sharers" in the Lord Chamberlain's Men. He had invested money in it to pay for costumes, playbooks and the wages of actors and stage hands.

17. Anti-Stratfordians were the people who believed that William Shakespeare from Stratford-upon-Avon could not have written his plays as his commonplace country background did not fit their image of the genius who penned the plays. The anti-Stratfordians believed that only an educated, sophisticated man of high social standing, like Sir Francis Bacon, Edward de Vere, Roger Manners or Sir Walter Raleigh could have written them.

18. In 1598, Globe, a theatre came into existence when the owners, the Burbage brothers, lost the Theatre's land lease. The land was not theirs but the building was. So they and their friends got together and dismantled every board and nail of it in the dead of the night. They carried the timbers over the frozen River Thames to Bankside and assembled a new building. Eight months later this furnished building was christened the Globe, the finest theatre that London had ever seen till then.

19. Following the death of Queen Bess, her cousin James, who was the King of Scotland, took over as James I of England. King James was a great theatre lover.

20. King's Men was the theatre company known earlier as The Chamberlain's Men. King James of Scotland on assuming the throne of England, after the death of Queen Elizabeth I, became a patron of Shakespeare's company and renamed it King's Men. King James's support came at a time when the theatre had to be closed down due to an outbreak of plague. The King's Men were issued a royal licence to perform seven of Shakespeare's plays at court between 1604 and 1605. The King's Men achieved unequalled success and became London's leading theatrical group.

21. New Place was one of the most prominent and desired properties in all of Stratford purchased by Shakespeare in 1597. It was the second largest home in Stratford belonging to a former Mayor of London. It had three storeys, five gables, more than ten fireplaces, gardens, orchards and a chapel. It indicated Shakespeare's financial success attained from a lifetime of creative work.

22. In 1609, Thomas Thorpe, a London publisher, published a book called *Shakespeare's Sonnets* containing more than 154 sonnets of Shakespeare. These sonnets were addressed to an unidentified young nobleman and the remainder of which speak of a "dark lady". The published sonnets were addressed to "Mr W.H.", which gave rise to the theory that the young man was Henry Wriothesley, Shakespeare's patron, whose initials H.W. are W.H. in reverse.

23. As with all aspects of Shakespeare's life, the facts are not clear. The thirty-six plays published in the *First Folio* are mostly agreed upon. *Pericles* was published later, as was *Two Noble Kinsmen*, which Shakespeare is believed to have contributed to. Including the controversial lost *Cardenio*, this brings the potential total number of plays to thirty-nine.

24. One of the factors may have been his huge vocabulary. His words contained some 30,000 words compared to just 3,000 used by the average adult today.

25. This line was written by playwright Ben Jonson to describe his friend William Shakespeare and how right he was. Over the years, styles of

acting and staging plays have changed many times but Shakespeare has not gone out of fashion. His plays have been translated into almost every language and are still performed all over the world.

26. Shakespeare's best known early tragedy is *Romeo and Juliet* in which two young lovers are kept apart by a bitter feud between their families. The others are *Hamlet, Othello* and *King Lear*. *Hamlet* became famous for Prince Hamlet's soliloquies on the meaning of life.

27. In 1623, Henry Condell and John Hemminges, fellow actors of Shakespeare, published thirty-six of Shakespeare's plays in the leather-bound book called the *First Folio*. A folio from the Latin word for 'leaf' is a large book with pages made up of standard sheets or leaves of paper folded in half. This was published seven years after Shakespeare's death in a single volume "only to keep the memory of so worthy a friend and fellow alive, as was our Shakespeare", to quote Condell and Hemminges.

28. William Shakespeare's plays became notable for their use of soliloquy, in which a character makes a speech to himself or herself, so that when the play is staged, the audience can understand his or her inner motivations and conflicts. Among Shakespeare's most famous soliloquies is the line uttered by the tragic hero Hamlet, "To be, or not to be…", meaning that Hamlet is wondering whether to live or to die.

29. William Shakespeare died on April 23rd, 1616, a month after completing his will. He was buried at the Holy Trinity Church in Stratford with the words, "Curst be he that moves my bones" inscribed on his grave.

30. William Shakespeare's knowledge of men and poetic skill combined to make him the greatest of playwrights. His plots alone show that he was a master playwright. He developed his plays with care and seldom wrote a speech that did not forward the action, develop the character or help the imagination of the spectator. He wrote his plays for everyday people keeping in the mind the fact that many in the audience were uneducated. The public looked up to him as a funny, exciting and loveable entertainer, not as a great poet or an actor.

OTHER HARDBACK BOOKS

» 1984 by George Orwell
  Fiction/Classics, ISBN: 9788193545836
» Abraham Lincoln by Lord Charnwood
  Biography/Leaders, ISBN: 9789387669147
» Alice's Adventures in Wonderland by Lewis Carroll
  Children's/Classics, ISBN: 9789387669055
» Animal Farm by George Orwell
  Fiction/Classics, ISBN: 9789387669062
» Gitanjali by Rabindranath Tagore
  Fiction/Poetry, ISBN: 9789387669079
» Great Speeches of Abraham Lincoln by Abraham Lincoln
  History/General, ISBN: 9789387669154
» How to Stop Worrying and Start Living by Dale Carnegie
  Self-Help/General, ISBN: 9789387669161
» How to Win Friends and Influence People by Dale Carnegie
  Self-Help/Success, ISBN: 9789387669178
» Illust. Biography of William Shakespeare by Manju Gupta
  Biography/Authors, ISBN: 9789387669246
» Madhubala by Manju Gupta
  Biography/Actors, ISBN: 9789387669253
» Mansarover 1 (Hindi) by Premchand
  Fiction/Short Stories, ISBN: 9789387669086
» Mansarover 2 (Hindi) by Premchand
  Fiction/Short Stories, ISBN: 9789387669093
» Mein Kampf (My Struggle) by Adolf Hitler
  Biography/Leaders, ISBN: 9789387669260
» My Experiments with Truth by Mahatma Gandhi
  Biography/Leaders, ISBN: 9789387669277
» Relativity by Albert Einstein
  Sciences/Physics, ISBN: 9789387669185

OTHER HARDBACK BOOKS

» Selected Stories of Tagore by Rabindranath Tagore
   Fiction/Short Stories, ISBN: 9789387669307
» Sense and Sensibility by Jane Austen
   Fiction/Classics, ISBN: 9789387669109
» Siddhartha by Hermann Hesse
   Fiction/Classics, ISBN: 9789387669116
» Tales from India by Rudyard Kipling
   Fiction/Short Stories, ISBN: 9789387669123
» Tales from Shakespeare by Charles & Mary Lamb
   Children's/Classics, ISBN: 9789387669314
» The Art of War by Sun Tzu
   Self-Help/Success, ISBN: 9789387669321
» The Autobiography of a Yogi by Paramahansa Yogananda
   Biography/General, ISBN: 9789387669192
» The Diary of a Young Girl by Anne Frank
   Biography/General, ISBN: 9789387669208
» The Jungle Book by Rudyard Kipling
   Children's/Classics, ISBN: 9789387669338
» The Light of Asia by Sir Edwin Arnold
   Religion/Buddhism, ISBN: 9789387669130
» The Miracles of Your Mind by Joseph Murphy
   Self-Help/Success, ISBN: 9789387669215
» The Origin of Species by Charles Darwin
   Sciences/Life Sciences, ISBN: 9789387669345
» The Power of Your Subconscious Mind by Joseph Murphy
   Self-Help/General, ISBN: 9789387669222
» The Science of Getting Rich by Wallace D. Wattles
   Self-Help/Success, ISBN: 9789387669239
» Think and Grow Rich by Napoleon Hill
   Self-Help/Success, ISBN: 9789387669352

Get 25% off on Amazon.in | Search the book by its ISBN

www.ingramcontent.com/pod-product-compliance
Lightning Source LLC
Chambersburg PA
CBHW030502100426
42813CB00002B/310